"Sam Jones inspires me not only as a barbecue man, but also as a person. Whole hog is considered by everyone who cooks barbecue to be the most challenging meat to master, and Sam Jones has it mastered. Sam is one of the best barbecuers living; he is also a great storyteller, and *Whole Hog BBQ* is a cookbook and history book that teaches you how to cook whole hog and all of the other fixings that have made the Jones family famous. Sam Jones and his book are authentic, and represent what is great about barbecue."

—TUFFY STONE
five-time Barbecue World Champion
and owner of Q Barbeque

"This book is a beautiful journey through an incredible family history. Sam Jones is simply the finest of humans and I'm blessed to call him my brother."

—BILLY DURNEY
chef/owner of Hometown Bar-B-Que

"Sam Jones is a barbecue unicorn. He makes my favorite barbecue in the state of North Carolina, and he occupies a space that few others can, as both an heir to the traditions and legacies of the past, and a diplomat and forward-thinker for the future of the craft. His reputation for incredible barbecue is exceeded only by his reputation for kindness and generosity."

—ASHLEY CHRISTENSEN
author of *Poole's* and chef/owner
of Poole's Diner

"Great storytellers are as rare as real barbecue pitmasters. While some spout their credentials and accolades like a metronome, Sam Jones humbly captivates your attention with a symphony of gritty, emotional stories and the knowledge of a three-generation barbecue family. Sam Jones is a rarity."

—CHRIS LILLY
pitmaster and partner at Big Bob Gibson Bar-B-Q

"As I write this, I'm sitting at a block pit, cooking a hog. It's just me and Sam, and it's 2:12 in the morning. There are a lot of folks out there who romanticize this lifestyle, but very few of us who live it. Sam is someone who lives this lifestyle. The procedures and recipes in this book are so steeped in culture that I promise you will feel that culture as you cook through this book. Sam's a great cook and a legendary pitmaster, but he's an even better friend. I know I'm biased—but you will be, too, when you read through these pages."

—PAT MARTIN
owner of Martin's Bar-B-Que Joint

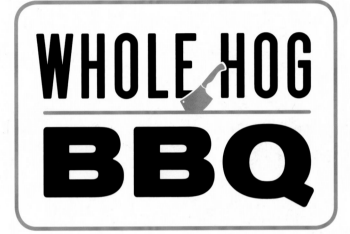

The Gospel of
CAROLINA BARBECUE
with Recipes from
Skylight Inn & Sam Jones BBQ

Sam Jones & Daniel Vaughn

PHOTOGRAPHS BY DENNY CULBERT

ILLUSTRATIONS BY JEB MATULICH

TEN SPEED PRESS
California | New York

CONTENTS

INTRODUCTION

NOTES FROM SAM JONES 1

One

SKYLIGHT INN

Jones BBQ Gospel

Sweet Coleslaw 37

Old-Fashioned Cornbread 38

Eastern North Carolina–Style
Chicken and Sauce 41

Home-Style Potato Salad 44

Mama's Banana Pudding 47

Two

THE WHOLE HOG

Block Pits and Burn Barrels

BQ Grill vs. Block Pit 57

Choosing a Hog 58

Throwing a Whole Hog Party 60

Equipment and Ingredients 62

Timeline for a Noon Whole Hog Party 87

Three

SAM JONES BBQ

Third-Generation Perfection

Rub Potion Number Swine 127

Sweet Barbecue Sauce, aka "Bean Sauce" 128

Eastern North Carolina Barbecue Sauce 129

Pork Spare Ribs 131

Smoked Turkey Breast 133

1947 Burger 136

Hog Head Collards 139

Barbecue Baked Beans 143

Pimento Cheese 146

Sweet Potato Muffins 149

Four

PIT RESURRECTION

Feasting on Tradition

Shrimp Stew with Scallops 167

Fish Stew 171

Country-Style Steak and Gravy 175

Cabbage Collards 176

Pig Pickin' Cake 180

Biscuit Pudding with Chocolate Gravy 185

Resources 189

Acknowledgments 191

Index 197

NOTES FROM SAM JONES

I stood over a once-forgotten pit that had been in my family for almost a century. It hadn't been warmed by wood coals for at least six decades. We had missed out on so much potential camaraderie, food, and joy while it sat dormant, and I felt honored to resurrect it on a chilly March morning in 2018. The hogs on the pit were whole, and the fuel was nothing but hardwood. The hog cooks who came before me wouldn't have had it any other way, and neither would I.

The men who dug this pit are long gone, but I hope somewhere they were nodding their affirmation, or at least an acknowledgment that I hadn't yet screwed up the family barbecue legacy. The steps I took to cook the hogs that day in March weren't any different from the ones they would have taken a century ago. It's further gratification knowing that the hogs in my restaurant today are being cooked with the same fundamental barbecue principles. My granddaddy Pete Jones always said, "If it's not cooked with WOOD it's not BBQ."

What is barbecue? That depends on the cook you're asking, I reckon. Ribs might be on the lips of a Memphian, Californians might say tri-tip, and in Kansas City they'll be arguing about sauce. A Texan will surely tell you that it's not a barbecue joint without brisket on the menu, but in my mind, barbecue is whole hog cooked over wood. I say that because I was raised in eastern North Carolina, and that's all we've ever done. East of Interstate 95, that's the expectation. That's how my family, the Joneses, have been doing it at Skylight Inn in Ayden, North Carolina, since 1947.

Over time, that definition of North Carolina barbecue has been diluted so that any tender pork that's chopped with vinegar is considered barbecue, even when it's done without a stick of wood. I think of that as cooked pork, and some of it's dang tasty, but it's not what I consider to be traditional North Carolina *barbecue*. In my opinion, cooking over wood is the essence of traditional barbecue, but only a handful of old-school places do it like I think it ought to be done. One of the newest in that mix is my restaurant, Sam Jones BBQ, in Winterville, North Carolina.

In eastern North Carolina, more so than anywhere else in the country, the definition of barbecue has historically been pretty simple: a whole animal cooked over wood, or coals. Long before the days of butcher shops and barbecue joints, this is how barbecue was cooked, be it whole lambs, goats, small steers, or hogs. It was done that way out of expediency when the slaughter was part of the barbecue event, and meat didn't arrive in a refrigerated truck. It just so happens that we still think it's the best way. I personally don't believe you can re-create what happens when you cook a whole animal if you start with an individual cut. All the muscles, and fat, and skin combine to create a mixture of dark and light meat, of lean and fatty meat, which can't be matched by a pork butt or a ham. Then, if you make the mistake of cooking without wood, there's nothing you can do to make up the ground you lost in flavor, no matter how much sauce you add.

I'm a product of that barbecue, having eaten it all my life. I'm also a product of my community and my state. There's always a Yeti cooler full of Cheerwine, the beloved cherry-flavored soda and North Carolina's finest elixir, in the back of my Super Duty pickup. My truck is equipped with the lights and sirens required for it to double as an emergency vehicle because I happen to be the fire chief in Ayden as well. The irony of my two callings being building fires and putting them out isn't lost on me. We average about three hundred calls per year out of two fire stations, which are made up of volunteers. We get a stipend of nine dollars per call. We obviously don't do it for the money.

That also means that my wife, Sarah, needs to worry about two different kinds of fire taking me away from home. She's the person who holds our family together when I'm gone for a week at a barbecue festival in New York, working long hours at the restaurant, or leaving in the middle of the night for a fire call. Funny enough, our first date was over barbecue, but it wasn't from the Jones family.

You see, my family is known for barbecue. I'm the third generation of Joneses to own a barbecue joint. I'm also the first who hasn't had to farm tobacco. I still support my forefathers' efforts with a Marlboro Light habit I need to let go of, but the tobacco barns are fewer and farther between in North Carolina these days. In rural, eastern North Carolina, the current cash crop is pigs. There are more pigs than people in the eastern part of

the state. We go through seventy of them every week between Skylight Inn, owned by my dad, Bruce Jones, and Uncle Jeff Jones (who's really my dad's cousin and not my uncle, but that's what I grew up calling him), and Sam Jones BBQ, which Michael Letchworth and I opened up the road in 2015. The two restaurants are seven miles door-to-door from one another, and worlds apart in how they're operated. They're still joined by one important commonality, and that's whole hog barbecue cooked over wood.

That's why that first date with Sarah back in 2006 was a little awkward. We went with a group to Parker's Barbecue in Greenville, about twenty minutes north of home. She knew I was in a funk, which I'll explain later, when she called me and said, "Hey, I've got some family coming in town and they want to go out to eat." I won't ever forget. I was at home sitting in my barn when she texted me and said, "Everybody's going to Parker's. Would you like to go?" I was like, "Yeah, I might."

I drove separate. I told her when I pulled up in the parking lot, "I believe I'd rather get caught selling drugs as to be in Parker's. Somebody's going to see me in there and decide to be a comedian." The door hadn't closed behind us as we walked in there when I heard, "Oh, you come to get some *good* barbecue, did you?" That's the way it is in a small town, especially when your family owns another barbecue joint. The little bit of embarrassment from that night was worth it, though. Twelve years later, Sarah and I have two daughters, Elaina and Eliza. They're not quite old enough to pick up a shovel, but one of them could be the family's fourth-generation pitmaster.

My family taught me everything they know about cooking whole hog barbecue, but they weren't very good at the teaching part. How many times has a barbecue cook been asked a question he didn't know the answer to? In my family, it's plenty of times. The answer is usually "Because we've always done it this way." To me that is not an answer. Just because you've been doing something for a long time doesn't mean you were doing it right.

Case in point: At Skylight we would cut cabbage for slaw on a prep table and rake the trash leaves into old bags. A couple of local guys would pick up the bags and feed the cabbage to their livestock. When we prepped the cabbage, one person would always walk down to the end of the table where that bag was tied to the corner and hold the bag open for the other one to rake the leaves in. It had been that way as long as I can remember. Mike "Chopper" Parrot had been at Skylight for two weeks. I was cutting cabbage, and I said, "Mike, will you hold that bag open for me?" And as I was raking them in there, Mike said, "This is stupid." He goes in the stock

Clockwise, from below: Jeff Jones, Bruce Jones, me, and Pete Jones in 2003 at the counter of Skylight Inn; Buddy Mills, Pete Jones, Kenneth Ross, and Bruce Jones with me in his arms in 1981; John Bill Dennis, Emmitt Dennis's brother, cooking a whole hog.

room, pulls down a cardboard box, rolls it up, slides it into the cabbage bag, then rolls it back out so the bag stands up on its own. I felt like the stupidest man in the world. So every day that we make slaw, you will see a cabbage bag with a piece of cardboard inserted in it. It stands on its own, and one man can do the job. That's the kind of simple innovation that can happen when you start asking if the way we've always done it is the right way to keep doing it.

Neither Pete Jones nor his brother and business partner, Robert, could read or write. They literally could not have put pen to paper to describe the details of making our slaw, cornbread, or the whole hog barbecue. Those are the three legs supporting the Jones family barbecue table. It would have never occurred to either of them to explain why any of the particular steps were necessary anyway. Because "that's the way we've always done it" was always explanation enough for them.

Take my granddaddy's morning routine. He would get up at 6:30 a.m. My grandmother would make coffee in a bubble-top pot. This makes no sense to me, but he poured coffee into a cup and set it on a saucer. He'd take the cup and saucer to the table, pick up the cup, and pour the coffee into a bowl. He'd blow on the coffee, let it cool, then drink it right out of the bowl. I have no idea why he had to mess up three dishes. He did it every day. In this book, I want to tell my story. I want to tell my family's story. I also intend to tell you when you can skip the cup and saucer and just go straight to the bowl. Whole hog barbecue takes a long time, but it's not complicated. There's no point in trying to make it more complex just so I come out looking like some kind of genius.

Whole hog barbecue might be simple, but it is never not a spectacle. As long as America has had hogs, we've had whole hog barbecue. And as long as hogs have cooked over coals, onlookers have stared longingly in amazement. When a whole hog is on the pit, people are drawn to the fire. They're drawn to the smoke. Droplets of fat explode into scented puffs of smoke that rise to flavor the pig and perfume the air. Down in the cooker, red hot coals peek out from under a blanket of ashes and send up ribbons of shimmering heat. It's hard even for me not to stare, even after all these years of cooking.

Once we flip the hog, the skin becomes the focus of the cooking. If whole hog is the old testament of barbecue, it's that shatteringly crisp skin that is the gospel according to the Jones family. Crowds gather to look on as the hog is lifted from the pit and onto the cutting block. "Can I get some skin?" ask the uninitiated, who don't realize how important it is to our finished product. We chop it right into the meat.

In eastern North Carolina, for a handful of barbecue joints, this spectacle is a way of life. Skylight has been giving pit tours probably since it opened more than seventy years ago, and our pit-house doors are always wide open to visitors at Sam Jones BBQ. We have nothing to hide, and frankly we're proud to show the place off.

Creating that same spectacle in your own backyard isn't out of your grasp either. You might have seen the high price tags of sleek offset smokers used to cook brisket in Texas or the stainless steel rotisseries for ribs in Kansas City, but to do whole hog right, all you need are some concrete blocks, some sheet metal, and an old fifty-five-gallon drum. I'm going to show you, every step of the way, how to build the pit, harvest the coals, and slowly cook a whole hog at home. Think of this book as the quickest way to make yours the most popular backyard in the neighborhood.

We'll begin with my family's barbecue history, which eventually led to my grandfather Pete Jones opening Skylight Inn, and my father, Bruce Jones, along with cousin Jeff Jones and me, continuing the legacy today. I'll share recipes for some of our most famous items and the methodology behind our whole hog barbecue. The second section

focuses on how to re-create that whole hog magic just about anywhere that can accommodate a pallet full of concrete blocks. A more expansive barbecue menu can be found at Sam Jones BBQ, and you'll be able to make most of it from recipes in the third section. The final portion of the book reveals family recipes that have previously been held so close to the vest that I didn't even know how to make them. Now, you'll also be able to celebrate like a Jones.

Barbecue has always been about community for the Jones family. Every community is woven together like a blanket. I think every business and family that is a part of a community, especially a small community, is automatically a part of that woven blanket. You have to choose if you're going to be a strong thread or the weak one. If we hear of a death—not only in our community, but maybe you were a patron of ours, and your father passed away—we're going to send a spread of barbecue and sides to your house from both restaurants. I'll try to carry it myself if I'm home, because it's something that's important. Also, because I know what it means to be that person on the other end. We've learned a thing or two about building bonds by building barbecue pits. Build a block pit in your backyard, and you'll be surprised how quickly and easily you can bring a community together. That's the power of whole hog.

One

SKYLIGHT **INN**

Jones BBQ Gospel

If you don't live in eastern North Carolina, and you've heard of Ayden, it's because of barbecue. More specifically, it's probably because of the whole hog barbecue at Skylight Inn. When somebody from Seattle or Sweden plots a barbecue pilgrimage to Pitt County because they saw Skylight on a television show or a barbecue best-of list, we have my grandfather Pete Jones to thank.

Pete Jones started building Skylight Inn when he was a teenager. At the time, he was working at the City Cafe, a country cooking place with whole hog barbecue run by Emmitt Dennis, one of Pete's uncles, in downtown Ayden. Emmitt taught Pete how to cook barbecue. While working for Emmitt, Pete also had plenty of responsibilities on the family tobacco farm. He was expected to be a part of the labor workforce, and that farm wasn't a big moneymaker. It was there to sustain the family. The family grew, and the mayonnaise doesn't spread but so far on the bread. In an effort to do better for his family, he went to the other side of town and opened Skylight.

At this time Pete's brother, Robert, worked for another family member also selling barbecue. He was Emmitt Dennis's brother, John Bill. Pete and Robert were as close as any two brothers I've ever witnessed. They became partners in the farming operation, and once the restaurant picked up, my grandfather needed to have less responsibility as it pertained to the farming aspect. They became business partners in the restaurant as well. Robert would tend to the farm, Pete would tend to the barbecue joint, and they'd split everything evenly.

Skylight Inn opened July 8, 1947. Barbecue was his main squeeze, but Pete had hamburgers, hotdogs, and whatever else a burger joint might have on the menu. With two other places selling barbecue in town to compete against—his uncle Emmitt's City Cafe *and* his other uncle John Bill's place downtown—he needed to set himself apart. Pete never drank, but Skylight served beer, had a jukebox (which also played through outside speakers), and was open as late as 11 p.m. I've heard stories of my great-grandmother firing a shotgun in the air from her porch across the street and shouting, "It's time to shut it down." Young couples and fellas with their mistresses would park behind the restaurant, and they weren't there for the barbecue. One could say it was a bit of a wild place in the beginning.

Pete was ready to build a dance hall out by the pack house, sort of beside the restaurant. He had it staked off and everything. Both of my great-grandmothers on this side of the family were churchgoing women, and both of their husbands were drunks. As I said earlier, granddaddy never drank, but he didn't attend church back then. The preacher came out to see him one day to tell him the dance hall wasn't the right thing to do. If I had to bet, it was something along the lines of how that dance hall would upgrade his ticket to hell to first class. Ole Pete told the preacher that he wouldn't tend to the church's business, if the preacher would let him alone to tend to the barbecue business. That was right before my dad got run over the second time. We'll get to that story in a minute, but it gave my granddaddy a change of perspective. He never did build the dance hall, and by the late 1950s, Skylight stopped selling beer. In 1971, the town of Ayden issued a curfew due to civil unrest, so Skylight started closing up at curfew, 7 p.m. It was then that Skylight Inn ceased being a late-night hangout spot and became a full-fledged barbecue joint.

The original smokehouse was a cinder block building with a dirt floor. The pit was made of regular brick, and it had just a small chimney. A big day back then was three hogs, and hundred-pound ones at that. That's about all that would fit on the pit. They raised their own hogs in the early years, and not because they wanted to be trendy. They were farmers. They were raising them anyway, so might as well cook the ones they had.

Thus far it may seem they lived a nostalgic country life. The Joneses did not have that life. My granddad had a wife and two children, a brother with a wife and four kids, and a sister and brother-in-law with one. The significance of me telling you this is because at one point, each family lived in the same house that Pete's mother fired that shotgun from. My dad's bassinet was a dresser drawer by day. They had nothing, but it wasn't because anyone was lazy—they were just dealing with hard times.

There were an especially bad six years when my father was just a kid: six years of bad harvests, six years of little rain when the crops needed it, and too much when they didn't. Then there were the enormous medical bills from my dad's close brushes with death as child. I'll let him tell you about them in his words:

I've been run over twice. I was four the first time. I was riding with my granddaddy on a two-ton truck, standing in the seat with a balloon hung out the window. The door came open when he turned the corner. I fell beneath the truck and the back wheels got me. I broke everything on the right side of my body—arm, ribs, leg, and foot. The doctor fixed me up. I was in a body cast for months.

The second time I was seven. I was holding hands, as our mothers told us to, with my first cousin Jeff. We were crossing the street to get to Skylight. I was just ahead of Jeff, and I didn't see the car. Still holding hands I got hit at one driveway and got knocked down to the next driveway. Jeff did not. It was worse than the first time. We didn't have a rescue squad. The hearse from the local funeral home carried me to the hospital. The funeral director, Jimmy Farmer, told my daddy, who was not a church man at the time, "Get anybody who knows how to pray, I'd get them started. I don't think your boy will make the ride to the hospital."

I made it to the hospital. The doctor told daddy, "I can't set any bones until he regains consciousness, and I really don't think he's gonna regain consciousness." Mr. Farmer, who had picked me up in his hearse, sat there all night long. Daddy told him he appreciated it, but there was no need in him staying at the hospital, but he said, "Pete, I don't mean to be ugly or cruel for you, but from what the man said, it would be a waste of my time to go to Ayden and have to turn around and come back." I didn't get back in that hearse. The same doctor that fixed me up at four did it again.

The doctor told daddy, "Now, we've done the surgery on your boy. It's been a success, but in the long run, this boy is not going to be able to walk the cement floor. He's going to have to have a sit-down job." My daddy told him, "There ain't no sitting-down jobs in the barbecue pit or the farm. Sorry."

It took a long while to heal, but I laugh when I tell people now. I'm sixty-seven, still walking the floor of the barbecue place. There's been no sitting down on the job.

My granddaddy Pete and his brother Robert weren't selling enough barbecue to cover for the tobacco losses. All the businesses in the community would let their neighbors buy on credit. This was the norm for our area, as there were so many who farmed. They would just carry your bill all year, and you made sure to pay up after the harvest came in. Pete was no different and had to negotiate that. Pete would go to these places and say, "Look—I don't have any money. If you work with me, I'll make it right." He had to do that for six straight years. Pete eventually paid his debt, but it's crazy to think that Pete owed these folks for six years.

For six years asking the men who owned the fertilizer company for more credit. Mr. Thelbert Worthington, who owned Worthington's Five & Ten, allowing clothes and school supplies to walk out the door with the Joneses, yet they had no money to pay. McDonald Edwards, who ran Edwards Pharmacy, allowing medicines for all those kids, one of them crippled, to be prescribed with nothing in return. Pete didn't pay those people a dime in those six years, but they still carried him.

When I started working at Skylight Inn, three or four guys would pull up by the back door in their nice car on Saturday mornings. My granddad would make somebody, oftentimes me, stop what he was doing to go see what those guys wanted. I did it one Saturday, and a guy in a Cadillac wanted two pounds of barbecue and a piece of skin, which we do for nobody. I was thinking, "There's a line of people inside. Why do I need to stop working to go out here to provide this special service?" Pete said, "Get the man whatever he wants." Then, we didn't even charge him.

Pete wasn't known for doing anything extra for customers when we were busy. He put paper trays of slaw in to-go bags because he was too cheap to buy a container with a lid. He would actually argue with you if you just wanted to change your order, so I was wondering, "Who is this guy?" It bothered me enough to ask my dad. He told me the man I carried food to was McDonald Edwards who used to own Edwards Pharmacy. (I still get my prescriptions there today.) Another gentleman was Thelbert Worthington who owned the five and dime. These were the guys who carried Pete through those rough years.

It was this community that allowed Skylight and the Joneses to survive, which gave us the opportunity to thrive, and for the Skylight name to become a legend. Well, maybe for Pete Jones to become a legend, anyway. There are still customers who call it "Pete Jones Barbecue," and he's been out of the business since 2004. I reckon they may not even know it's called Skylight, which, admittedly, isn't a name that exactly screams "barbecue." It came from a local pilot who flew over the place while it was under construction. He observed from above these apparent holes in the roof. This was obviously a question he needed answering, so after he landed in the small airfield behind the property, he walked over and asked my granddaddy if he had planned to put skylights in the roof. A conversation was had about it, and somewhere in this exchange, the name "Skylight Inn" was born. At least that's how the story has always been told to me. Then again, our family stories aren't short on embellishments.

The last photo of Pete Jones at Skylight Inn, taken two weeks before his passing.

The Pete Jones mantra: "If it's not cooked with WOOD it's not BBQ." He didn't mind saying it, because that's exactly what he believed, and more than a little bit strongly. The haphazard piles of split oak wood out behind Skylight are a testament to that. We go through it too quickly to bother with stacking.

The mantra was at the front of Pete's brain when some out-of-towners walked through the door in 1979. They were from *National Geographic*. A writer, Thomas O'Neill, and photographer Ira Block were trekking across the country stopping in small towns researching for a book that would be named *Back Roads America*. O'Neill wrote that the day they visited Skylight Inn they were on "a search for the best barbecue in eastern North Carolina." When they told Pete of their quest, he simply said, "You've come to the right place."

He explained to them the importance of wood cooking and demonstrated it by having an employee fetch a plate of gas-cooked barbecue from a nearby restaurant. There was no comparison. "So I called off my search," said O'Neill, who was so thoroughly impressed with granddaddy's whole hog that Skylight was his only stop for barbecue.

If you've researched the history of Skylight Inn, so much of our story is wrapped up in that visit from *National Geographic*. Every explanation of the silver dome . . . oh yeah, there's a silver replica of the US Capitol building on top of Skylight's roof. Pete built it four years after *National Geographic* declared Skylight Inn the "capital of barbecue." Years ago, you would hear me telling the story often, and so many reporters have repeated it that it might as well be fact. My dad will tell you that Pete never boasted about his barbecue until *National Geographic* called it the best in the country—except they never really said that.

To understand how significant the *National Geographic* mention really was, remember that back in 1979, pork fat was the enemy. It was surprising that anybody wanted to do a story about pork barbecue. When the folks from *National Geographic* came in, I think it was probably the first experience of anybody from outside the area giving a damn about Skylight. As with the first customer at a child's lemonade stand, my grandfather shifted to into sales-pitch mode. I say that because ole Pete handed them a shirt with "AYDEN, BAR-B-Q CAPITAL OF THE WORLD" printed on the front. Meaning, he was so certain of his own barbecue he had printed a shirt before *National Geographic* ever walked through the door.

I know he received a copy of the book, *Back Roads America*, when it came out. Due to Pete not being able to read, somebody, most likely my grandmother Lou, would have had to read it to him. The words "Bar-B-Q Capital of the World" are printed on the page, but only to repeat the boast on Pete's shirt. No matter what the book really said, it changed everything. It had been a long time since day one in 1947. This was the first blip for him on anyone's radar. He, and the family, had worked every day, all day, and finally someone noticed.

The local newspaper reported on the newly minted barbecue capital. Pete Jones was heralded as a barbecue king. It was now his job to make it true, and he did. The wood fires never ceased, and new customers looking to knock him off the throne would be their own judge. They couldn't argue after a bite of Pete's barbecue. As he told *People* magazine in 1989, "If a man has but one item to sell, it has to be good." With wood-cooked whole hog and a little exaggeration, Pete built his own kingdom, one persuaded customer at a time.

Pete's inflated claim of barbecue dominance also lit a fire in my dad. Bruce, who by then was working full time at Skylight, learned of the 1981 Barbecue Bowl taking place in Washington, DC. One North Carolina representative was challenging another from South Carolina about which state had the better barbecue. North Carolina's representative was Gene Johnson from Greensboro. Bruce called him to share the *National Geographic* story, or at least the story as recounted by Pete, and told Mr. Johnson that Skylight needed to be part of the Barbecue Bowl. Here's how Bruce told it to me:

I called Gene Johnson in Greensboro and I said, "Mr. Johnson, I understand y'all are having a barbecue contest and you don't even have barbecue." He said, "Who are you?" I said, "Bruce Jones, Pete Jones barbecue." I didn't say Skylight Inn, I didn't start, but most people knew. He said, "Well, what makes you think yours is so hot?" I said, "*National Geographic* just featured my daddy"—the guys used the term "Barbecue King"—so I said, "featured us as the best barbecue in the nation right now." He said, "Really?" I said, "Yeah," and I told him about the article. He said, "Well, bring it to Washington." And so, by that time I hate to say I was the mouthpiece of the store, I come back and I tell Daddy, "Hey, we got a chance to go to Washington, DC."

That's one day that my dad stepped out to garner some attention in a way that Pete never would have. So Bruce and Pete packed up some freshly chopped barbecue into an insulated box and boarded a little Cessna. They flew to DC and served the barbecue at the Capitol. There's a photo of Bruce, Pete, and Strom Thurmond, at the time a senator from South Carolina, from the Barbecue Bowl, which was supposedly taken just after Thurmond abandoned a plate of South Carolina barbecue in favor of Skylight's. North Carolina governor James Hunt Jr. sent a congratulatory letter to "Barbecue King of the World," Pete Jones. Of course, that letter is still on display at the restaurant today.

If you're the barbecue capital, you might as well have a dome to match. At least that was Bruce's thinking when it came time for an expansion of Skylight in 1984. As he told it to me:

I said, "Daddy, since you have been recognized, or referred to as the Barbecue King, let's put a dome on the top and be the Barbecue Capitol." I said, "Come on, it'll be unique." Larry House built it for us. When he first built it, it looked like a church steeple rather than a dome. It made him mad when Daddy said, "Tear it off." Daddy told him how he wanted it and Larry built it about half the size, and Daddy said, "Tear it off, it ain't what I want." On the third try, he finally built it like it is now. And it became a talk piece, you know, for a while people wanted to know, why the dome? And I said, "It's the barbecue capital."

Business was great then, and the accolades kept coming. *People* magazine said we had the best barbecue in the country in 1989. The *New York Times* praised it in 1995 almost as much as the *Washington Post* did five years later. They all mentioned the skin, which has been the signature of the Jones family barbecue.

Lots of barbecue joints discard the skin after cooking, or fry it up for cracklings. Part of our process has always been cooking the skin until it's crisp, then chopping it into the barbecue. There was a time when customers could ask for big pieces of skin on the side. But it became too popular, and there wasn't any skin left to chop into the barbecue. That's when Pete starting chopping it all into the barbecue, and now it wouldn't be Jones barbecue without it.

I grew up on that pork skin. My dad jokes that he even added a little pork lard into my baby bottles to be sure it was in my blood. I was raised working in barbecue. Not just in barbecue, but in my family's barbecue place. One of my first duties working at Skylight was to weigh in the hogs. A man named Floyd would deliver the hogs, and they came tagged with a weight. There's a set of scales with a hook just outside the cooler door where the hogs were hung to double-check their weight. I would slide a cinder block over and stand it up the tall way so I could reach the scale to verify the weight. I didn't realize it then, but even at a young age, I was partially responsible for the profitability of the restaurant on some level.

That restaurant—it wasn't just a place to make money. Don't get me wrong, Pete enjoyed making money. But it was always something more than that. He gave birth to that child. He struggled for decades through its slow growth, so when it came to flourishing, it was like Pete was watching his child walk across the stage during graduation.

I used to think he was the craziest man in the world, because the few days that we were closed in a year, he would still be at the restaurant. It would come time to eat Thanksgiving dinner (that would be lunch to some), and my grandmother would look to me and my cousins and say, "One of you boys step across there to the restaurant and tell your granddaddy to come on, it's time to eat." I'd walk across the street, and I'd see him watching me. He knew I was coming, and he knew why, but he'd stand right there, propped up on one elbow, smoking a cigarette, and gazing through the front double doors until I walked in and the doors closed behind me. The place was closed, but that's where he wanted to be. I often wonder, what was he thinking about? Probably imagining a line of customers standing there and converting his barbecue into their cash.

I was sitting in the doctor's office with a cold on June 4, 2004. My aunt brought Pete into the same office with chest pains. The next thing I knew they had called the ambulance, and Pete was on his way to the hospital. As always, my dad was at church. I called my mom, because he doesn't use a cell phone, to tell him he needed to come to the hospital. He and I went in the back of the ER where they were about to rush Pete away for a heart catheterization. He told my dad, "Until I can get back on my feet," pointing at me, "let Samuel take care of the pig bill," and this and that. He lived for almost two more years, but following that procedure, his mind was never the same.

A few months before his heart attack, he shared with me some things that I then wrote on a napkin—for example, the arrangement we had with the family we buy our pigs from. He said, "I might not be around here forever and somebody needs to know a few things." As I said before, my crowd are awful teachers, so it wasn't like he gave me a detailed orientation about how to run Skylight, but it was something. I mean, nobody else had made decisions in that place while Pete was around. He was much like the mafia dons of the past: nothing happened without his blessing.

My granddaddy never returned to retake the throne, or even walk through the smokehouse to see if things were going like he wanted them to. The few times he came back in, he would be escorted by his caretaker, and most often the visit he demanded to have would be cut short due to his mental status. Looking back, I wonder, do we work away the best years of our life, then die? Shortly after his exit, we had three people quit. I had to hire three people to replace them, and one of them was Michael Letchworth. When Pete came in and saw those three new people, he surmised that they'd been hired to do the work he had been doing. Or, in his lingo, "Yep, took three people to replace me."

Pete passed away February 15, 2006, about two years after his heart attack. After the funeral, when the funeral procession left the church on the way to the cemetery, the hearse stopped in front of the restaurant, which of course was closed. It was just a pause, maybe thirty or forty seconds, then the hearse picked back up again. A sign taped to the restaurant's glass door announced matter-of-factly, "Pete Jones Died." No other explanation was required other than when we would reopen.

My dad preached the funeral. He is the pastor at Kings Cross Roads Free Will Baptist Church in Fountain, North Carolina. That is just outside Farmville, which is a small town of about five thousand, northwest of Ayden. My dad is one of those folks who is going to church one more time after he dies. That's just how it is. He once said, "I'm a preacher who's a barbecue man," and not the other way around. He tends to be a matter-of-fact guy.

A lot of folks thought the barbecue at Skylight would never be the same. Even though Pete hadn't lifted a shovel in ten years or better, apart from cooking the hog he gave to the family that now tended the farmland. (That was a tradition he started years after he and Robert retired from farming, and one we still follow today.) Plenty of customers had convinced themselves the barbecue took a nosedive after Pete died. Rumors circulated that we had sold the business or were planning to. None was remotely close to the truth. However, perception is a powerful thing. It led to some rough years at Skylight. We weren't starving to death, but the pig bill that was usually reconciled on Sunday sometimes had to wait until Monday or Tuesday for our sales to catch up to our debts. Still, we never let go of Pete's barbecue commandment. "If it's not cooked with WOOD it's not BBQ." That is the one thing he did show us how to do.

The challenges back then weren't just monetary, either. When Pete passed on, I was still recovering from a tragedy that had rocked my life a year prior. On August 15, 2005, I picked up my longtime girlfriend, Ashley Farmer, to go to the evening church service, just like I had so many times before. There was an accident, and we didn't make it to church. I was just twenty-four years old, and my life changed irreversibly that day.

Perception and perspective can be equally powerful. The perception we have of other people's lives in this age of social media is often shaped only by the positives. Whether it's an athlete, movie star, singer, or even a celebrity chef, it's easy to think they have it made and don't suffer from the same afflictions that we all face, especially when they only post images of the good life. But the truth is, we're all just people. We all have the same vulnerabilities and insecurities. And once you've lived through enough of those difficult circumstances, you gain perspective.

Ashley and I went to dad's church back then, and I will never forget the sermon from the first service that day, entitled "Trials of Your Faith." Bruce talked about how faith wasn't faith until it had been tested. When the invitation was given, I walked down to the altar. I was moved, and had finally realized she was my person. I wanted to go thank God for her, and didn't yet know how significantly my faith would be tested.

We left church. I dropped her off at her home, then picked her up later for the evening service. We were both laughing as I drove down the same route we always took. I pulled into an intersection, and my truck was struck on her side, ejecting both of us from the vehicle. I came to, face down on the highway. Ashley was under the hood of my overturned truck about forty feet away, upside down. As I crawled to where she was, I managed to find my portable radio for the fire department. I called in the accident, and I knew, based on my training, she was not in good shape. We had been laughing on our way to church at 6:20. At 6:36, she was gone, but I didn't yet know as I was being placed in an ambulance.

The doctors and my dad kept the news from me in the emergency room. My test results came in just before midnight. The doctor said he would discharge me, but only after I had been told. In my room, I asked again how she was doing and my dad looked at me and said, "Son, Ashley didn't make the ride."

Two days later, I stood bruised and bandaged in front of a casket holding the twenty-one-year-old young lady I loved. The following weeks, months, and years were the hardest and darkest I've ever experienced.

It seemed in a short while everyone else's world started to spin again except for mine, and her family's. Faith in a brighter tomorrow and the friends who rallied around me are the only reasons I believe I'm here to share these words. That same small community that sustained my family decades prior did the same for me in a completely different way.

Earlier, I told you about that first date with Sarah, but here's the full story. When I was dating Ashley I didn't know Sarah. She ran a hair salon in town, and she had been Ashley's stylist. The day after the accident, my dad took me to Ashley's house to mourn with her parents, Russell and Sandra, and her sister Jessica. Both of our houses were full of people from the community. We retreated to a back bedroom and cried, but as soon as we gained our composure, her mother looked at me and said, "Samuel, we have a funeral to plan, and you need to be a part of it." We decided her girlfriends would pick her outfit and I said, "We should ask the Whaley girl if she would do her hair and makeup." Sarah agreed, but refused any compensation. A month later, out of loyalty, I felt obligated to go to her to get my hair cut.

I still hadn't emotionally recovered from the accident when Sarah called me to eat barbecue a year later. We joke now about it being our first date, but neither of us saw it as a date back then. We did start dating soon after, and got married in the fall of 2007. We have two daughters, Eliza, who is eighteen months, and six-year-old Elaina, who is in kindergarten. I've learned that making it through life's challenges provides the tools to take on the next one. That event helped change my whole attitude on life, and my perspective on the lives of others. I'm now more prone to empathize than to judge. The things that used to get me bent out of shape are trivial to me at this point. Weathering the storm makes one appreciate the rainbow all the more.

•   •   •

It was 2008, just before noon on a hot August day in Pitt County. You could just about stare at something hard and set it on fire. Maybe someone had, because there were about 150 acres in flames, a pretty good-sized fire, in the woods a few districts away, but close enough that we got a call for help. By "we," I don't mean Skylight. I mean the Ayden Fire Department, where I was assistant fire chief. So we sent an engine, a brush truck, and ten of our men.

Later that afternoon, my chief called me to say that they still needed more manpower. It crossed my mind that while we're paying so much attention to first and second base, so to speak, we might also want to think about home plate. After all, it was hot at home, too. And barbecue happens to involve a fair bit of fire. However, we sent a few more men after giving our roster a quick rundown. At this point, we had only six able-bodied firefighters left in Ayden, not including a few of the older guys who primarily drove the trucks. It was pretty slim pickings.

Back at Skylight I was fully aware of the conditions on all fronts. It was super hot, with low humidity, just right for the smallest of sparks to cause a big problem. I just didn't realize it would be *our* problem. James Howell, who at that time was the main man in the cookhouse and had been tending the pits for decades, was about to leave for the day. I told him to make sure not to leave anything burning in the chimney when he closed up the smokehouse for the night. Normally there might be a few pieces of wood burning up there and it wouldn't be a big deal, but that day . . .

Shortly after six that evening, and almost immediately after James had locked up, I saw the smoke through the window. Growing up in a barbecue restaurant gives you some particular powers of perception when it comes to reading smoke, and it was immediately clear to me that this wasn't pig-cooking smoke. It was the other kind. The kind I learned about in my fire training. I did some sort of an Ayden high-step as I charged through the kitchen and out the back door into the yard to realize my truck was in danger. I moved it, took off my apron, and jumped into my turnout gear like Superman in a phone booth. As I ran back toward the cookhouse, I called in to our 911 center from my portable radio: "4221 to Pitt County; I'm on scene and establishing Skylight command."

I grabbed an old rickety stepladder that you wouldn't use to cross a ditch, and set it up next to the smokehouse, which was fully and truly now on fire. As I watched flames shooting about three feet above the ridge vent along the full length of the roof, I gave a thought to James, he of few words, and wondered if he'd made it home yet. The doors to the smokehouse were locked (and I didn't want to open them anyway—it'd only feed the fire), so I got a hose from behind the building and told one of the employees to crank the water on. I aimed and prepared to suppress the fire that was currently turning our business into smoke.

I swear, a man on dialysis has more pressure than what came out. So much for Superman.

By then, even the power line to the smokehouse had burned in half and was jumping all around on the ground, arcing everywhere. It was dire.

Live-fire training exercise just east of Ayden.

Fortunately for me and the Skylight, some of those last able-bodied men down at the station had an engine on the scene in about four minutes, with the police not too far behind. And the local news. And some customers. Even with the fire trucks and squad cars on-site, we had a man come in and ask for two pounds of barbecue, bread, and slaw to go. I finally had to have someone go inside and lock the door.

James came back the next day. He didn't have much to say.

We started tearing the roof off—Uncle Jeff and I did the demolition ourselves to save money. It's not like we had $20,000 squirreled away for just such an occasion, but we rebuilt. The fire inspector called and told me I could borrow his pig cooker if I needed it. We had the doors back open on Saturday.

I replaced the ladder.

Business got better. Some of that press we'd received in the early '80s came trickling back starting in 2008 when the Southern Foodways Alliance made a film about Skylight Inn called *Capital Q*. We hadn't even rebuilt that pit house. They later asked me to attend a showing of the film at the Big Apple BBQ Block Party in New York City.

Attendees were mesmerized by the double cleavers chopping whole hog on a big wooden block. They laughed when my dad said our barbecue was the King James version of barbecue, and I retold the *National Geographic* story. I also told the story of Skilton Dennis, my great-great-great-great-grandfather. He was part of another one of those family legends, about a man selling barbecue in 1830 out of a covered wagon in the middle of Ayden, a legend that had been passed down within the family just like gospel. It's a story I never questioned until I took a trip to a cemetery.

There's not even a path to the Dennis Family Cemetery in Ayden. A few broken gravestones sit among a stand of trees in the middle of a field. You can only get to it when the crops are out of the field. I went to find a trace of the man who had served barbecue out of the original food truck in 1830. I found Skilton Dennis, but he was born in 1842. I found his mother, Mantha Dennis, too. Back at home, I scoured the genealogy sites for Skilton's father, Skilton Sr. What I learned was that Mantha's maiden name was Dennis. She never married. Young Skilton took his mother's name, and his father was never mentioned, and no other Skilton Dennis was listed in the census.

We don't know if the younger Skilton was in the barbecue business, but he was certainly in the pig business. He also had some impressively large daughters, according to the *Eastern Reflector* newspaper. On May 7, 1884, they printed:

> I understand that Skilton Dennis, of Contentnea Township, has two daughters, 15 and 13 years of age, weighing 200 and 240 pounds, respectively. Skilton is a good, sober Democrat, who raises plenty of hog and hominy.

As with the *National Geographic* story, Pete Jones had made the legend of the older Skilton Dennis true. For festivals and catering gigs, Pete had served barbecue out of a replica covered wagon with "Since 1830" painted on the side. Enough reporters had repeated the story that it had become fact. The story was one Pete had likely heard from his forefathers and simply repeated to a willing audience who always loves a good backstory. Nobody back then had access to the digital records we can now access with a few clicks.

Even without the covered wagon in 1830, it's still one heck of a family barbecue legacy, which continues beyond seventy years and into the third generation. That's a lot longer than most barbecue businesses last.

Pete Jones's covered catering wagon in front of Skylight Inn, before expansion, in the early 1980s.

Skilton Dennis's tombstone at the Dennis Family Cemetery.

It's the legacy that once prompted the author Michael Pollan, who was searching for a barbecue joint to feature in his book *Cooked*, to say: "I was looking for the most unreconstructed cooking I could find, cooking as it's been practiced for thousands if not millions of years, and I found that in Eastern North Carolina whole hog barbecue."

It's the legacy that embraces myth and can will Ayden into becoming the "Bar-B-Q Capital of the World." Was Pete Jones a talented enough cook and showman to make everyone believe stories like those? Yes—absolutely.

I don't consider myself any type of big shot in the barbecue world or the food world. We're just a family that got fortunate enough that what we do became popular. It was good and people liked it. We were able to make a living. I don't think barbecue is one of those things where there's always got to be a cool, new kid on the block or whatever. Maybe in other foods, people forget the old places while in search of the new star, but I hope barbecue never evolves into that. We've been doing it this way all along because it's what we believe to be the right way even though it also happens to be the hard way. Another family member may come along after I'm long gone and find that cutting corners is worth the extra sleep or the extra profit. That's not gonna happen while I've got a hold of this torch.

From left: Me, Bruce Jones, and Jeff Jones in the doorway of the Skylight Inn pit room, aka the Vestibule of Hell.

SWEET COLESLAW

Makes 8 to 10 servings

A barbecue sandwich in Ayden is only a barbecue sandwich if there's slaw on it. It's automatic. Our slaw is a simple mayo-based slaw that is sweet and heavy on the dressing. When I say sweet, I mean that we don't even let salt and pepper get in the way. My favorite part of the slaw is the juice that pools on the top of a batch after it's been mixed. I could drink it by the cupful, so I don't like a slaw that's not juicy.

Our slaw is so finely chopped, you could call it minced. It's chopped in an industrial-size Hobart grinder, twenty heads of cabbage at a time. At home, you could hand chop the cabbage, but the minced texture is probably best achieved after a few pulses in a food processor.

The flavor of cabbage changes throughout the year. In the spring, the heads are fluffy. As the year goes on, they get denser, and the flavors are more concentrated. Uncle Jeff calls that "spicy cabbage," and it tastes a little like horseradish. Don't worry, as the sweet dressing mellows it right out.

When I was a child, my dad, who is a Baptist minister, left to go to church one evening. A guy who works for us walked up to me and said, "Hey, man, we're about out of coleslaw." I thought that wouldn't be much of a problem, if only I knew how to make it. I called my dad on the phone, and everything he told me was "about." Put about this of mustard, and put about that of mayonnaise. I thought there was no way I was about to get this slaw right, but I guess the good Lord was smiling upon me. We made it and it tasted right. The lesson there is that it'll be fine as long as you get it "about" right.

1 head cabbage, about 2½ pounds	¼ cup salad dressing, such as Miracle Whip
1¼ cups sugar	2 teaspoons yellow mustard
⅓ cup mayonnaise	

Quarter the cabbage by cutting down into the core. Turn each quarter on its side and cut down the edge of the solid core to remove and discard it. Peel off the outer leaves and discard as well. Cut into 1-inch chunks and, working in batches, fill a food processor with cabbage to the halfway point. Pulse six times, then run the food processor continuously for 30 to 60 seconds until the cabbage is finely chopped. Stop short of a minced paste. Chopping by hand is possible, but the texture will be a bit bulkier. Start by cutting each quarter into thin slices against the grain of the cabbage. Stack the slices three or four high and slice thinly again, against the grain of the leaves. You should be left with fine bits of cabbage.

Place the chopped cabbage in a bowl large enough to allow some serious mixing.

In a separate bowl, mix together the sugar, mayonnaise, salad dressing, and mustard until fully combined. Pour over the chopped cabbage, mix well, cover with plastic wrap, and refrigerate. This slaw is best once it sits for several hours (that's when the precious juice rises to the top), but it's also ready to eat immediately if need be. The slaw is best the day-of because it loses its crispness overnight, but it will keep in the refrigerator for 2 days.

FOR A WHOLE HOG PARTY
Makes 70 to 80 servings

20 pounds cabbage	1¾ cups (14 ounces) salad dressing, such as Miracle Whip
4 pounds sugar	
3 cups (24 ounces) mayonnaise	2 ounces yellow mustard

OLD-FASHIONED CORNBREAD

Makes 12 servings

When I was a boy, the commodity hogs were fatter. A cut pan (I don't know why this round aluminum pan had that name) was put under a finished hog to catch the grease when it was quartered. The pan held about two gallons, and we'd need to change it out after three or four hogs. That's a lot of lard.

Today, we get our lard from the slaughter-house. It's not the hydrogenated stuff from the grocery store shelf. But if you don't have access to good lard from a local butcher, strained bacon grease will also work.

We use two stands, which are just shy of four gallons, of lard a week at the restaurant, which is about sixty pounds. Our cornbread recipe calls for four ounces of lard per pan. We still put a pan under the hogs to catch the fat when we quarter them on the pit. The collected fat is strained and added to the lard that we have to buy, but it's not even a quarter of the lard we need.

The hushpuppy mix we use is Moss Light n' Sweet Hushpuppy Mix with Onions from Buffaloe Milling in Kittrell, North Carolina. It's available online or on store shelves in Virginia and North and South Carolina. Moss's blend uses flour and cornmeal, like just about any other hushpuppy mix out there, so feel free to substitute. Just make sure there's a bit of salt and sugar in the mix, and add a teaspoon of onion powder if it's missing from the one you choose.

3 cups white cornmeal
2½ tablespoons hushpuppy mix
½ teaspoon salt

3¼ cups water
¾ cup lard or bacon grease

Preheat the oven to 400°F.

In a large bowl, stir the cornmeal, hushpuppy mix, and salt together. Add the water slowly while mixing and combine thoroughly. The goal is a batter that's the consistency of a thin pancake batter. Add more water if necessary to achieve this.

In a medium saucepan over medium heat, melt the lard. Pour it into a 9 by 13-inch pan, coating the bottom and sides, but *do not pour off the remaining lard*! Pour in the batter. The fat will come up around all the edges. It might look wrong, but that's the goal.

Bake for 35 minutes, until the cornbread is golden brown on top. Be careful of the hot liquid fat in the pan when pulling it from the oven. Serve immediately or within the hour. If you keep this overnight, you could probably use it to shingle a house. I don't recommend it.

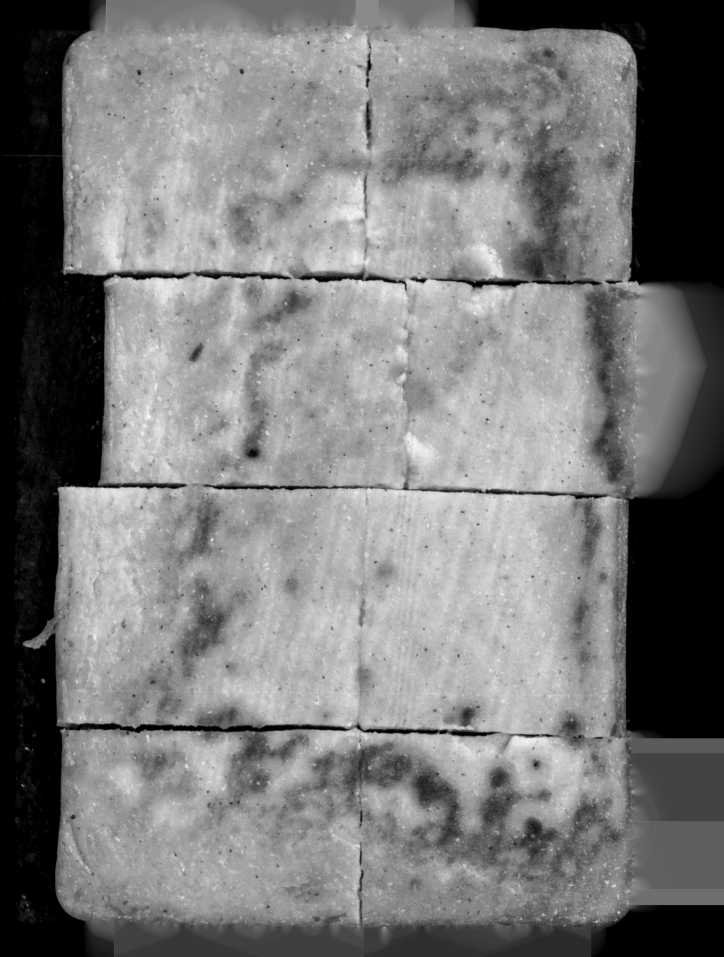

EASTERN NORTH CAROLINA-STYLE CHICKEN AND SAUCE

Makes 8 servings

This most recent addition to the Skylight menu came—against Bruce's wishes—in about 2010. It's hard to understand, but sometimes folks don't want whole hog barbecue. I hate to say it to the barbecue purists, but this chicken is more about the sauce than the chicken. We cook it over wood coals on the pit unadulterated, then it gets a bath in our chicken sauce, which is a sweet vinegar and mustard sauce.

We have a similar item on the menu at Sam Jones BBQ, but we do it a bit differently: the chickens are brined and cooked the exact same way, but they are rubbed liberally with Rub Potion Number Swine (page 127) before cooking, and we don't serve them with a sauce. Do it either way you like, or go crazy and do both the rub and the sauce.

Brine

1 gallon water

1½ cups sugar

1 cup kosher salt

1 gallon ice

Chicken

2 whole chickens, about 3½ pounds each

Chicken Sauce

½ cup sugar

¼ cup canned pineapple juice

3 tablespoons yellow mustard

½ teaspoon chili powder

2 cups ketchup

1 cup apple cider vinegar

½ cup Pepsi

¼ cup Texas Pete Hot Sauce

1½ teaspoons soy sauce

1½ teaspoons Worcestershire sauce

1½ teaspoons lime juice

1½ teaspoons lemon juice

To make the brine, in a 10-quart pot, bring the water to a boil, then turn off heat. Add the sugar and salt and stir until dissolved. Pour in the ice to chill the mixture. If you'd rather not bother with the ice, make the brine with 2 gallons of water, and do it far enough ahead so it will be completely cooled before adding the raw chicken.

To prepare the chicken, split each bird open at the breast rather than down the backbone. I guess you'd call it reverse spatchcocking. We do it that way because that's the way we've always done it. Sorry, I'm not completely immune to such reasoning. Submerge the chicken in the brine and refrigerate, covered, overnight or for at least 8 hours.

Heat a pit or smoker to 250°F. Remove the chicken from the brine and pat dry with paper towels. Discard the brine.

> Note: If you'd like to replicate the chicken from Sam Jones BBQ, at this point, apply about 1 tablespoon of Rub Potion Number Swine (page 127) to each side of the chicken. Sprinkle it all over the skin of the chicken and inside the cavity.

continued

Place the splayed chickens bone side down on the pit, directly over the coals. Let them cook for about 60 to 70 minutes, then flip the birds. It will take about 60 more minutes on this side, depending on the size of the chickens. Remove the chickens from the heat when the internal temperature is 165°F.

To make the sauce, whisk together the sugar, pineapple juice, mustard, and chili powder in a 4- to 5-quart saucepan over medium heat.

Add the remaining ingredients and mix well. Turn the heat to high and bring to a boil. Just after the sauce reaches a boil, remove from the heat. Allow the sauce to cool slightly and transfer to a heatproof serving bowl.

To serve, quarter the chickens, arrange on a serving plate, and cover with the sauce. Serve additional sauce in a bowl on the side. Of course, at Sam Jones BBQ we don't bother with the sauce.

Sam Jones BBQ chicken, just right.

Overcooked and scorched!

HOME-STYLE POTATO SALAD

Makes 6 to 8 servings

This is a classic Southern potato salad recipe with mustard *and* mayo. There are no herbs or celery, but you will need some pickles for this one. The "sweet salad cubes" called for in this recipe might not sound familiar if you're not from eastern North Carolina, but they are just sweet pickle relish that's not chopped fine. Sweet pickle relish will also work here.

2½ pounds russet potatoes, peeled and cut into ¾-inch cubes

Salt

½ cup sweet salad cubes or sweet pickle relish

4½ teaspoons diced pimentos

1 tablespoon finely diced green bell pepper

4 hard-boiled eggs, peeled and finely chopped

1 cup mayonnaise

4½ teaspoons yellow mustard

Place the potatoes in a large pot of water and season with salt. Bring the water to a boil and continue to boil for 8 to 10 minutes, or until the potatoes are fork tender. Drain the potatoes and set aside.

Drain the salad cubes and pimentos, discarding the juices. Place in a small bowl and combine with the bell pepper, eggs, mayonnaise, mustard, and ½ teaspoon salt. Mix well.

Pour the dressing over the potatoes, preferably while the potatoes are still warm. Fold the dressing into the potatoes (don't mash the potatoes) until well combined. Serve warm, or if your crowd is averse to potato salad that's not cold, chill in the refrigerator for a few hours. The potato salad will keep in the refrigerator for 3 days.

FOR A WHOLE HOG PARTY

Makes 70 to 80 servings

20 pounds russet potatoes

4 cups (32 ounces) sweet salad cubes or sweet pickle relish

6 ounces diced pimentos

½ cup finely diced green bell pepper

30 hard-boiled eggs, peeled and finely chopped

8 cups (64 ounces) mayonnaise

¾ cup (6½ ounces) yellow mustard

2 tablespoons salt

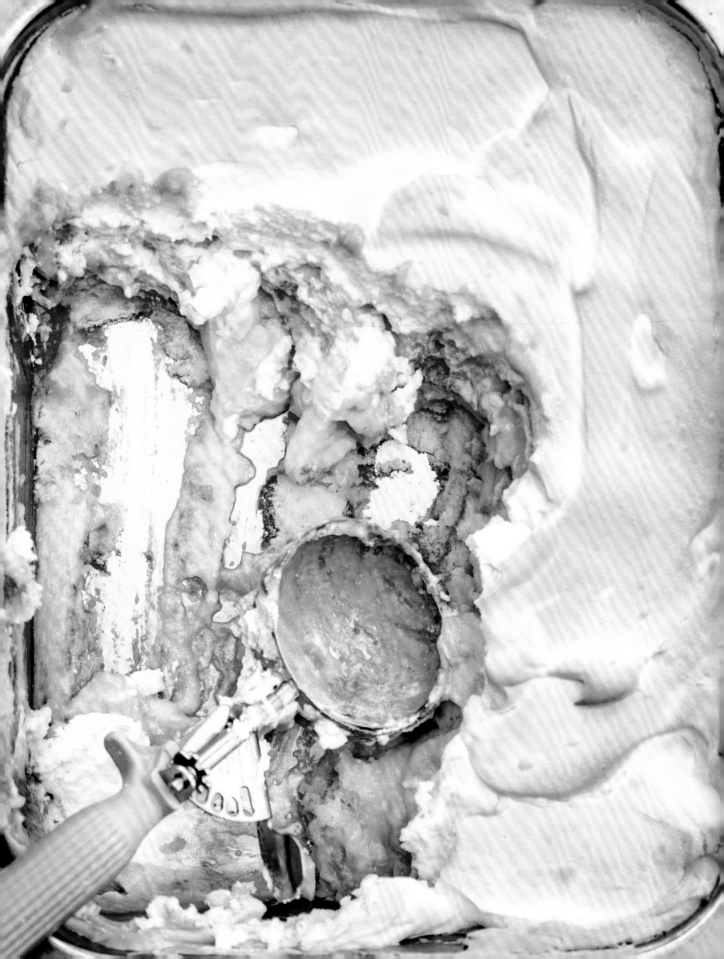

MAMA'S BANANA PUDDING

Makes 10 to 12 servings

This is my mother's recipe. It's so good you'll want to rub it on your face. When I was a teenager, at the homecoming lunch at church she'd always bring a big pan of it, because all the guys my age would target it. They'd go get a scoop of banana pudding before they'd get the rest of their food. It's famous in Pitt County, North Carolina.

14 large eggs, separated

3½ cups whole milk

1¼ cups all-purpose flour

2¾ cups sugar

1½ teaspoons vanilla extract

1 (15-ounce) box Nilla wafers

5 bananas, peeled and sliced

Preheat the oven to 375°F.

Place the egg yolks in a 5-quart pot. Off the heat, gently break the yolks with a fork, then add the milk, flour, 2 cups of the sugar, and the vanilla. Whisk together and place on the stovetop over medium heat. Bring the mixture to a simmer, stirring, for about 7 to 8 minutes, or until it thickens enough to coat the back of a spoon. The mixture will stick to the bottom of the pan and burn easily, so stir continuously. Remove the pudding from the heat.

Whip the egg whites in a stand mixer with a whisk attachment, or with a hand blender with a whisk attachment, until soft peaks form. Continue whipping while slowly adding the remaining ¾ cup sugar. Whip until the meringue has stiff peaks.

Layer half of the wafers on the bottom of a 9 by 13-inch pan. Pour half of the pudding over the wafers, spread out with a spatula, and layer with half of the banana slices. Repeat the layers. Top with the meringue, spreading it evenly. Bake for 4 to 5 minutes, or until the meringue is lightly browned. Cool slightly, but it's best served warm or at room temperature. Leftovers can keep in the refrigerator for a day or so, but the meringue will get soggy after a while.

Two

THE WHOLE HOG

Block Pits and Burn Barrels

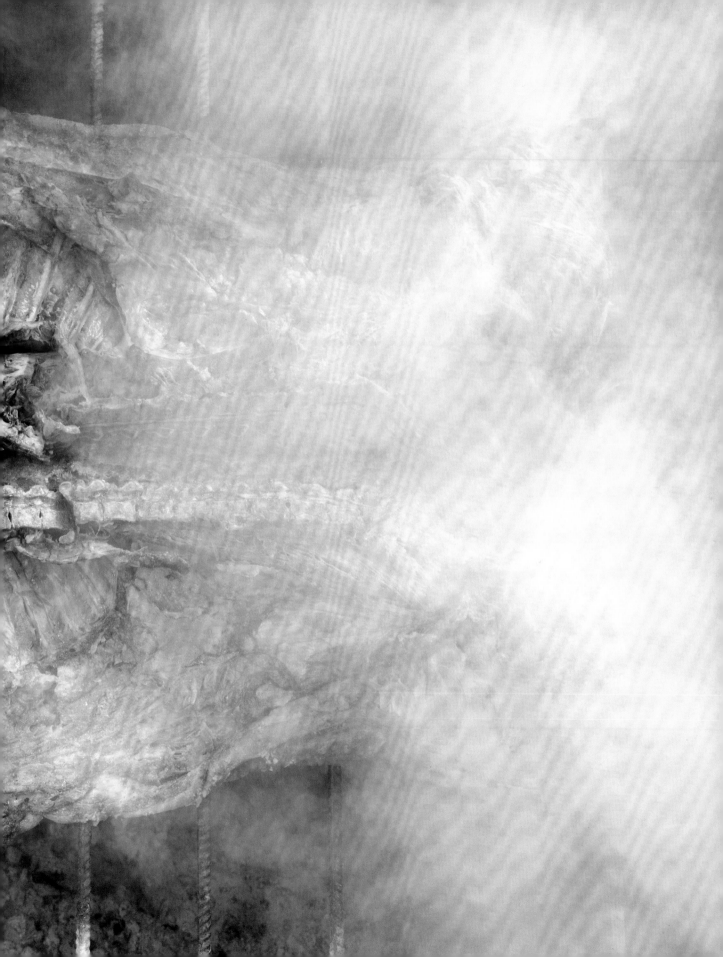

Cooking a whole hog doesn't have to be that complicated. If you heard that it's dang near impossible to get right, that's the difference between somebody talking about it who does it versus somebody who doesn't. It's a long process, but with a pickup truck and the right guidance, you could be serving one tomorrow.

You don't even have to stay up all night to cook a whole hog. At our family restaurants, we back up the start time and leave about five hours of extra cooking time. If a hog takes a little longer to finish than we'd anticipated, there's no need to rush it with that sort of a cushion. On the other hand, if we underestimated how many hogs we need for the day, or a local decided last minute he needed half a hog when we open the doors, we can push one and get it done in ten hours.

We do everything by temperature. It takes the art out of it. People can romanticize about cooking by feel, but any dummy can cook a great hog if they pay attention to the progress on a meat thermometer. We have talented people working the pits, but we also have new folks who are years away from knowing how to cook by feel.

The timeline we use at Skylight and Sam Jones BBQ is a sixteen-hour process for a 180-pound pig. It's intentionally dragged out to allow for sleeping soundly between about midnight and six in the morning. If you don't mind a sleepless night, you can condense the whole cook to as little as ten to twelve hours, depending on the size of the hog. Or, of course, if you're having hog for dinner, you can start early in the morning and have it ready by evening. I like to leave myself at least fourteen hours to have a buffer of an hour on each end. The timeline we use at the restaurants may vary depending on the time of year and whether or not the pit is already hot, but what follows is the basic procedure.

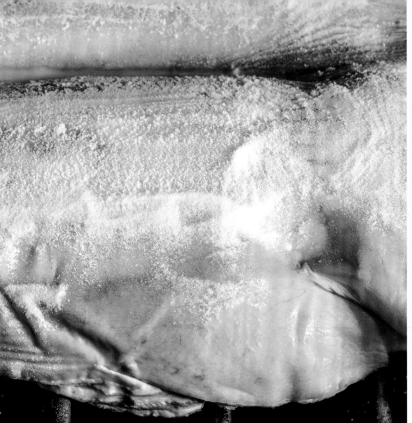

To start

We light a fire to make wood coals early in the morning. We call it the feeder fire, and it will stay lit all day long, which is what gives our pit room the affectionate nickname of "The Vestibule of Hell." Even when the fire goes out at night, the chimney never fully cools down. At home, you should plan to light the fire an hour before you start cooking.

3:00 p.m.

The pig hits the pit, skin side up. The skin is dampened with water and is heavily salted. The pit may or may not be hot at that point, but it warms up quickly once you add coals and put the lid on.

Once the pig is on, and every 30 to 40 minutes after

A shovelful of hot coals is added down each side of the pit. We always watch the pit thermometer, which should be somewhere between 250°F and 275°F. Once the pit and the hog heat up, the temperature may ride right there for an hour or more, so coals can be added less frequently.

8:00 p.m.

The internal temperature of the meat at the thickest part of the ham (the back hip of the hog) should be 120°F to 130°F. We flip the hog and add one last load of coals to the pit, then close the lid.

11:00 p.m.

Someone from the staff swings in to check the pit temperature. He may have to add coals, or may simply stir the coals already in the pit to kick up the heat, or may do nothing.

6:00 a.m.

The pit cook arrives and builds the feeder fire.

7:30 a.m.

Coals from the feeder fire are hot and ready. They're added to the pit to bring the temperature up to 250°F. The hogs are mostly cooked by this point, so this brings the internal temperature, which has probably dipped to 140°F to 150°F, up to 180°F.

8:45 a.m. (Skylight), 9:45 a.m. (SJB)

The hog that went into the pit first is identified. It will be the first to go in the restaurant, so it's time to crisp the skin on that hog. Coals from the feeder fire are placed directly under the pig to complete the process slowly. At Sam Jones BBQ, the heat shields are removed from inside the BQ Grill to allow for direct-heat cooking. There aren't any heat shields to deal with inside the brick pits at Skylight.

9:45 (Skylight), 10:45 a.m. (SJB)

A sheet pan is placed under the hog, and the hog is cut in half along the spine, then quartered. Two of those quarters, or half a hog, are brought in, and the chopping begins so it's ready to serve when the restaurant doors open. From there, the remaining hogs will be brought in a quarter-hog at a time for chopping throughout the day. We stage the cooking of the hogs so that all are not ready at the same time. This ensures that the pig served at 3:00 p.m. is the same quality as the one served that morning.

10:00 a.m. (Skylight), 11:00 a.m. (SJB)

The restaurant opens.

3:00 p.m.

The process begins again with the next day's hogs.

7:00 p.m.

Skylight Inn closes.

9:00 p.m.

Sam Jones BBQ closes.

BQ GRILL VS. BLOCK PIT

At Skylight, where I grew up, we always used pits built out of brick or concrete blocks. They work fine, but when I first took the barbecue show on the road, I needed a cooker that I could haul on a trailer, and concrete blocks weren't going to cut it. I sat down and kind of sketched out these steel hog cookers. I wanted to have a heat shield to deflect the drippings. If you have a fire, it's easy to put out and doesn't ruin the hog. I carried those sketches to Melvin Whitman at BQ Grills in Elm City, North Carolina, and he built a prototype. With a few tweaks, that's the design we cook with at Sam Jones BBQ. He and I are working on a few new ideas even now. A couple of those steel cookers may have crept into the pit room at Skylight as well.

People might try to crucify us for not building block pits, but what people need to understand is that I can turn out the same product in New York City on Madison Avenue on those steel cookers on wheels as I can in block pits in Ayden, North Carolina. To be truthful, I can do it better in the steel pits because I've got more elements of control. I've never cooked a pig in those steel pits and had a piece of meat that was scorched. Not a square inch of the hog was inedible.

The heat shield inside the steel pit also disperses the heat evenly. Cooking a hog over a hot bed of coals without that shield, you're going to have parts that need to be trimmed off. They just happen. There's nothing you can do about it. That's loss in the restaurant world. You're already behind in profit by using whole hogs because of how little of the hog you end up serving. If there's anything you can do to gain ground, you need to do it. It's also going to take less fuel to cook those hogs in a steel pit than it does in a block pit.

Now I'm not just in this business for the money, but a restaurant has to be profitable. It's hard enough to make decent money cooking whole hog barbecue over wood, which is one of the reasons it has been disappearing in eastern North Carolina. Hopefully, these steel pits will allow others to get into the business. Keeping a time-honored tradition thriving is only going to happen if folks can make a decent living.

If you're really dedicated to whole hog cooking, you can buy your own BQ Grill hog cooker, but of course, the benefit of a block pit is that you can build one in your backyard at a moment's notice for considerably less money. You just can't move it as easily when it comes time for say, an Easter egg hunt.

CHOOSING A HOG

Hog breeds are divided between so-called "lard hogs" and the leaner "bacon hogs." Lard hogs are robust with lots of back fat. When lard was a kitchen staple across the country, these hogs were prized for all that extra fat. This category includes breeds like the furry Mangalitsa and pudgy Ossabaw. Nowadays all that extra fat is used for making charcuterie, but it's not ideal for whole hog cooking. Much of the fat melts off and can become a dangerous accelerant, as I'll explain later.

Bacon hog breeds have more muscle and less fat, and are ideal for whole hog cooking. I've had success with Duroc, Red Wattle, and Berkshire breeds, but the most common one you'll find is the American Yorkshire. This lean hog with pink flesh dominates the commercial pork market in the United States, and is likely what you'll get if you order a hog from any old butcher. It's also the cheapest.

We have the benefit of ordering our hogs from a supplier called Bar-B-Que Pigs out of Wilson, North Carolina. We've been using them for decades, but you probably won't have the luxury of hog selection that we get, seeing as we're in the second-biggest hog-producing state in the country. If you have an Asian supermarket in your city, they probably have whole hogs on hand for sale. Any butcher worth their salt will be able to order one for you, but plan a few days in advance. If you have a producer near you that raises heritage breed hogs like Red Wattles or Durocs, you can ask them where you can purchase a whole hog. They may be able to get you a deal. Those same heritage breed hogs are now becoming easier to get in big cities with boutique butcher shops, but be prepared to pay a whole lot more, sometimes three times as much, as you would for a commercially raised hog.

When you figure out where to get a hog, be sure to request the following to save yourself some time: Ask for the backbone to be cracked, as this will allow the hog to lay flat on the pit. Keeping the head is optional, but recommended (you typically have to pay for the head, anyway). If you get the hog head-on, I would suggest having it partially split as well, for the same reason. If, however, you intend to use the head for seasoning or stock (see Hog Head Collards, page 139), you can leave it whole. Have the feet removed to allow for more space in the block pit.

THROWING A WHOLE HOG PARTY

Whole hog is an event. It's not just a meal or a cooking method. Meat cooked over wood is the most basic definition of barbecue, but a whole animal roasting over coals is more than just barbecue: it's a spectacle.

I was cooking two whole hogs in downtown Kannapolis, North Carolina, the home of the Gem Theatre and both Dale Earnhardts. The skinny: I was supposed to cook for about three hundred guests at an afternoon event for my good friend Vivian Howard at a premiere party for her show *A Chef's Life*. By the time it was all over, we'd only gone through one hog and had a whole one left. It was only about six in the evening so, we carried it to the after-party.

Later that evening, we all gathered in the bar at the Hilton Garden Inn. I had been back for thirty minutes or so when I went outside to smoke a cigarette and up pulled a white work truck. Vivian and the driver jumped out, and the three of us grabbed a tablecloth from the back of the truck. Inside was that leftover hog. We brought it right into the lobby of the hotel and sat it on the empty breakfast table. I was a bit worried, but the desk clerk checked with the manager to make sure nobody's head was going to catch fire—he walked up, studied the pig a bit, and said, "I reckon it'll be all right. Can I have a plate?"

So that's what happened: thirty of us standing around a pig on the hotel breakfast table, at midnight, at the after-after-party, just getting after it, true pig pickin' style. That's the power of the pig.

I routinely find myself in the midst of this spectacle while giving pit tours at the restaurants, working catering jobs, and serving barbecue fans at festivals across the country. It's a good feeling to make other people happy through barbecue, and honestly, it only takes a few trips to the hardware store and a stop at the butcher to make it happen in your own backyard.

Cooking a whole hog is more intimidating than it is difficult. But before you go out and buy a hog, remember that this is no small project. A 180-pound hog will feed about a hundred people. It is, however, worth noting that a whole hog party becomes easier by a factor of ten once the block pit and the burn barrel are in place.

Concrete blocks are the choice of itinerant whole hog pitmasters across the country for several reasons. They're cheap, very easy to stack up, and hold in heat far better than sheet metal. Building a burn barrel (a modified fifty-five-gallon drum) to produce wood coals may seem

like a luxury that can be skipped over. It's not. Besides providing hours of visual entertainment during the long cook, it produces quality coals rapidly. It's also more efficient than building an open fire, which gives you as much ash as it does coals, and don't even think about simply cooking with the heat of a big fire in the pit. The hog will be burnt before it's medium-rare inside.

If you've bothered to build a pit and secure a barrel, you might as well do it right. This pit is meant for *whole* hogs, not half hogs, not pork shoulders or butts. In a whole hog, the liquid fats from all over the body of the pig pool in the center, and the different flavors of those fats mix together. The pool of fat submerges the lean loins, so they cook confit style. All that flavor is trapped within the vessel of the skin. In a half hog, the fat leaks out. Besides, nobody ever says they're gonna "go half hog." We call this book "whole" hog for a reason.

You're going to hear a lot about the importance of crisp hog skin. It's the ingredient that sets our barbecue apart from other whole hog barbecue. The skin captures more smoke flavor than the meat, so doing away with it would be throwing away valuable smokiness. The crunch of the skin also provides some texture to the finely chopped pork. There's plenty of fat mixed in with the meat as it's chopped, but the skin also holds pockets of tasty pork fat that are only released when bit into. In Ayden, chopped pork without skin is like a Snickers without the peanuts.

Cooking a large whole hog like this one is a task for at least two people. My team, specifically Michael Letchworth and Mike "Chopper" Parrott, often works one-handed (because they're usually holding a beer), so reinforcements are often necessary.

To decide when to start your cook, see page 87 for a sample schedule.

EQUIPMENT AND INGREDIENTS

WOOD

¼ to ½ cord local hardwood
(see step 1, page 65)

THE BURN BARREL

Safety goggles

Gloves

55-gallon steel barrel

Drill with steel step drill bit

Reciprocating saw with an
8-inch metal-cutting blade

Shovel, preferably with a flat head
and long handle

5 concrete stakes, each ½ inch
thick and 24 inches long

Hammer

2 or 3 concrete blocks

THE PIT

80 concrete blocks

10 lengths of ½-inch (#5) steel rebar,
each cut 5 feet long

2 sheets of corrugated metal,
each 2 feet by 8 feet

Drill with ¼-inch bit

Grill thermometer with probe

HOG

1 whole hog, approximately
180 pounds, skin on, head optional
(see step 4, page 76)

Safety goggles

Reciprocating saw with an
8-inch metal-cutting blade

Extension cord

1-pound box iodized salt

2 pairs 12-inch heat-resistant gloves

Probe thermometer

1 large cutting board

1 chopping cleaver

Large tub or sheet tray

1 chef's knife or serrated knife

Large pan for serving

SEASONING

2 quarts apple cider vinegar

6 cups Texas Pete Hot Sauce

½ cup ground black pepper

¼ cup table salt

OBTAIN WOOD

Cooking a whole hog over wood coals requires a lot of fuel. Hardwoods like hickory, oak, and mesquite will work well because they produce good coals. I like to use oak because we have a lot of it around in eastern North Carolina. Maybe you've got mesquite covering your back forty, or you just cut down a hickory tree. Either will work, as will just about any hardwood I've ever come across.

You'll need a fire that burns for a dozen hours or more, so prepare accordingly. I've gotten away with using just a quarter cord, but you won't need to sweat it if you have a half cord. Besides, any leftover wood can be used for your next whole hog. After you make the burn barrel, stack the wood next to the barrel.

For the best results, be sure to buy dry hardwood. Dry wood means wood that was cut down about six months earlier. Newly cut wood is called green wood. If that's all you have access to, you can make it work, but it'll take some extra effort. The water has to be driven out of the wood before it starts to burn. To do this, get a hot fire going and stack the wood high on top of the burn barrel so the wood on top can dry out. You'll be able to hear the wood hissing and see the water bubbling out of the ends. Once enough water is driven out, the wood will light. Think of it as preheating the wood. Good, dry wood doesn't need to be preheated.

Wood can dry, or age, for too long as well. If it's rotted or soggy, or has the density of balsa wood, it won't make good coals. Not ever. Save it for a bonfire because all you'll get from it is ash and smoke.

If you don't have enough wood coals, or you're running low on wood, you can add what I like to call a bag of cheat. Once there's a good fire going in the burn barrel, throw a full bag of lump charcoal, paper bag and all, into the bottom of the burn barrel. The hot coals falling on the fire from above will light the paper bag and the charcoal within. You'll have a mess of hot coals in about fifteen minutes. Keep a bag handy. Getting the hog done properly is more important than being a purist.

BUILD THE BURN BARREL

Put on a pair of safety goggles and gloves. Remove the lid from the 55-gallon barrel, if it has one, and discard it. If it's a solid lid, drill a hole in the top of the barrel near the edge with the step drill bit. Make sure the hole is big enough for the cutting blade of the reciprocating saw to fit into. This will be your starting point to cut the top off with the reciprocating saw. Insert the blade into the hole, and cut close to the edge of the barrel, all the way around until the top is completely separated (1). Do not cut off the lip of the barrel as it will not hold up as well.

Lay the barrel on its side and draw lines for the shovel opening at the bottom of the barrel. The top of the opening should be just below the lower rib of the barrel. Use the shovel to determine the width of the opening. I usually end up cutting this opening twice because I forget to measure the shovel width. You can straddle the barrel and sit on it to hold it in place, but it's probably best to have a helper who is also wearing safety goggles. You can choose to measure twice, cut once, and all that.

Once the lines are drawn, drill a hole in each corner of what will be the opening. The solid barrel floor will be a bit higher than the bottom edge of the barrel, so make sure to cut this opening just above the actual floor of the barrel. Use the reciprocating saw to cut between the drilled holes (2, 3).

Turn the barrel upright to drill holes for the concrete stakes (or rebar, as pictured) using the drill with the steel step drill bit. This allows you to drill holes of various sizes with the same bit, and the need for that will become apparent a few steps from now. The stakes will slide in just above the lower rib of the barrel. They will hold the flaming logs above the bottom of the barrel. This allows the chunks of hot coals to fall between the stakes as the fire burns.

Drill holes for two perpendicular layers of stakes (4, 5). Three will make the bottom layer, and two more will run perpendicular for the top layer. Remember that the holes in one direction should be slightly higher than in the other direction so the stakes don't hit each other when you're trying to slide them through (6). The holes on one side of the barrel need to be large enough for the stakes to pass through. The holes on the receiving end should be slightly smaller (just don't push the bit through quite so far). The smaller holes will receive the pointed end of each stake. After a few whacks with a hammer on the flat end of each stake, the pointed end will be jammed in place for good.

Once all the stakes have been pounded into place, you have a barrel ready for making coals. This barrel is built to last and should easily survive through several cooks. Replace it once it cracks or holes appear in the sides. One great thing about the size is that the barrel fits nicely under the lid of the pit for storage.

Figure 1. BURN BARREL

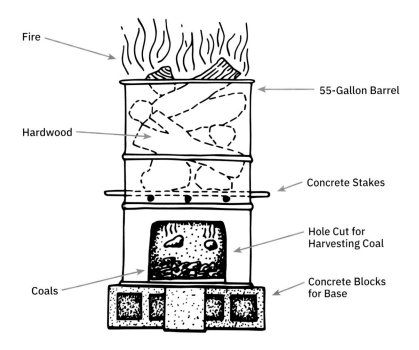

Fire

55-Gallon Barrel

Hardwood

Concrete Stakes

Hole Cut for
Harvesting Coal

Coals

Concrete Blocks
for Base

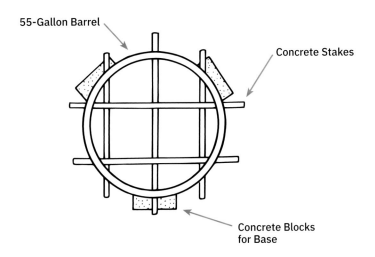

55-Gallon Barrel

Concrete Stakes

Concrete Blocks
for Base

Take two or three concrete blocks (you'll have a few more than you need for the pit) and make a base for the barrel. Stack wood into the top of the barrel and build a fire in the bottom. Cardboard boxes make good fuel for starting the fire, especially greasy pizza boxes. Once the wood above the stakes is lit, a load of wood coals is not far off. If it's a new barrel, the paint will burn off inside and out.

Don't let this fire go out. The coals you harvest from it are the only fuel you'll use to cook this hog. Keep loading the burn barrel and keep the fire going.

NOTE: Dress properly for whole hog cooks. There are sparks everywhere. If they land on your fleece or puffy jacket, those marks won't wash out. Wear flannel or a wool or canvas jacket that doesn't easily burn or melt. The sparks that don't land on your clothes and burn holes in them become ash dust, and it's everywhere. Wear light gray clothes and a hat to blend in, but you should still expect a few dandruff jokes.

STEP 3.
BUILD THE PIT

Find a patch of relatively flat dirt or lawn that you don't care too much about. It'll be green again in the spring if the pit doesn't become a permanent fixture. Build a base that's six blocks long on either side, with three blocks in between the long sides (1). Make sure the edges are straight and the corners are square.

Build a second layer with the blocks staggered over a half-block length from the first layer. A third layer follows, with the blocks staggered again to match the first layer (2, 3).

Lay the lengths of rebar going in the short direction and spread them evenly across the pit (4, 5). Now lay the fourth and final layer (staggering the blocks once again) over top of the rebar (6). Don't worry when the rebar keeps the top layer from sitting tightly against the layer below. Leaving the final layer of blocks out of one long side will make it easier to slide the prepared pig onto the pit.

> NOTE: If it's cold outside, the pit will benefit from a little preheating. Use the coals from the burn barrel to start a small fire right in the center of the pit. As it burns down, put the corrugated metal sheets on the pit as a lid to hold in the heat. Use the ¼-inch drill bit to drill a hole in the top of one of the sheets to accommodate the thermometer. Just before the hog goes on, scrape the coals used for preheating out to the edges of the pit. Then get a shovelful of hot coals from the burn barrel and spread them out to the edges of the pit.

Figure 2. BLOCK PIT

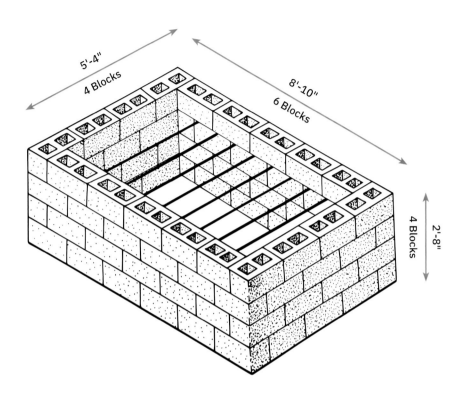

5'-4"
4 Blocks

8'-10"
6 Blocks

2'-8"
4 Blocks

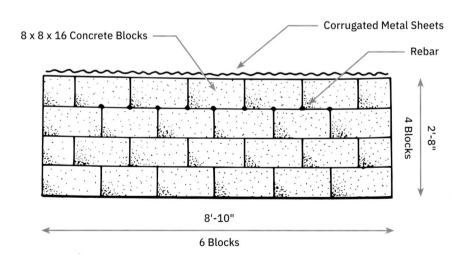

8 x 8 x 16 Concrete Blocks

Corrugated Metal Sheets

Rebar

2'-8"
4 Blocks

8'-10"
6 Blocks

Figure 3. PLAN OF FIRST BLOCK COURSE

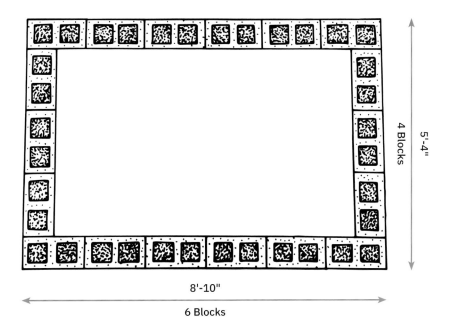

4 Blocks

5'-4"

8'-10"

6 Blocks

Figure 4. PLAN OF TOP COURSE WITH PIG

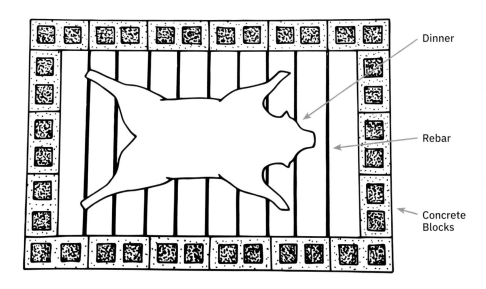

Dinner

Rebar

Concrete
Blocks

PREPARE THE HOG

You'll need to arrange the purchase of a whole pig. Any local butcher should be able to help, even if just to point you to someone who can sell one (see "Choosing a Hog," page 58). The size of the hog is usually based on the dressed weight (like the 180-pound hog mentioned here), not the live weight, but it doesn't hurt to clarify. Just as important is knowing if it will come frozen or fresh. Don't cook a previously frozen hog unless you have no other option.

We live in a state where you can't swing a baseball bat and not hit a hog, so procuring one isn't exactly a challenge for us.

Arrange a pickup time as close as possible to when you plan to start cooking, and bring a friend (or maybe two) with a strong back to help pick it up. The hog is not going to keep in your trunk for very long, and I doubt you have a fridge you can fit it in. And remember, it weighs 180 pounds. Plan accordingly when unloading the hog, and later when it goes onto the pit.

Set up a table long enough to accommodate the hog outside or in your garage. A six-foot folding plastic table works well. Clean the surface of the table, or cover it with plastic sheeting or plastic bags. Once the reciprocating saw is plugged in (get an extension cord long enough to reach the table), place the hog on the table, skin side down.

The following instructions may sound off-putting to some. Maybe you have a great butcher who will do it all for you, but I wouldn't count on it. When I travel to events, our team often communicates with whoever is ordering the hog. I request the proper preparation of the pig, and I even give detailed instructions, but it never, I mean never, shows up that way. Now, I encourage you to send these instructions to your own hog supplier, and maybe you'll get lucky, but it's probably safe to assume you'll have to do some of this yourself to make sure it's done right. It's time to roll up your sleeves and maybe even put on your trusty pair of safety goggles.

First cut the sternum to open the cavity fully. Now it's time to split the ribs apart. Basically, you'll make one long cut from the tail to the head. Start with the saw between the hams, about where the tail comes in. Cut through the spine, but not all the way through. It's important not to knick or cut the skin on the other side. The last thing you need is a drain for all the fat to run through.

Continue the cut along the spine and up between the ribs. Push down on the front legs to spread them apart. You'll hear some cracking. Keep cutting right through the neck and into the head. The neck meat is thicker than the back, so the blade can go a bit deeper. The head can be cut clean through or just enough so the hog splays out flat at the shoulders.

I cut the feet off because they get in the way during cooking, especially when it's time to flip the hog. Make a cut right through the joint just above the hoof. Discard the hooves or put them on the pit with the pig to make smoked trotters.

You can remove the head if you don't want to see it staring at you, but a pig will have died for your dinner either way. The pit size noted will accommodate a whole, 180-pound pig with the head attached. Use the smoked head for Hog Head Collards on page 139, or just dig into the tender cheek meat for an appetizer. The best few bites come from the head anyway.

When quartering the finished hog for serving, follow these lines. Start with a cut all the way down the spine, then separate one side between the tenth and eleventh ribs (start counting from the smallest rib toward the front of the animal). Chop and serve each quarter, then repeat the cross cut on the other side of the hog.

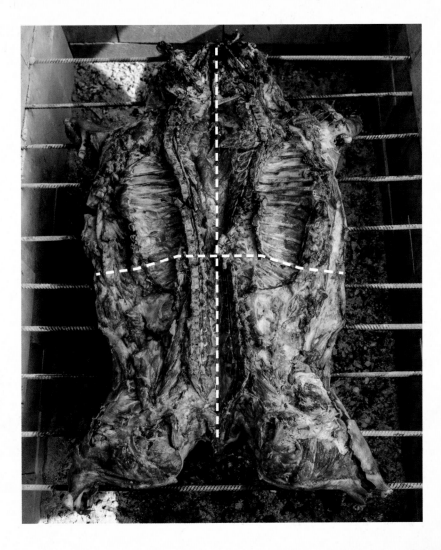

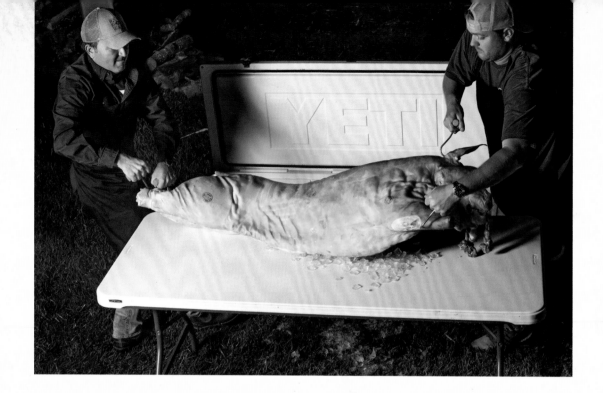

STEP 5.
COOK THE PIG

Task a friend or two with helping you carry the table and the hog over to the pit. This will be easier than carrying the pig itself. With a person on either end of the pig, lift it off the table by grabbing its legs, then flip it into the pit onto the rebar with the skin side up. If the pig is slippery, use a cloth or rag to help get a better grip on the legs. Once it's on the pit, pour water over the skin, just enough to wet the surface. Cover the wet skin liberally with iodized salt, but not so much that you have a solid layer of salt. One pound of salt should be about right for a 180-pound hog, and should be applied as evenly as possible.

Wash down the table the hog was just sitting on. Clean it thoroughly with soap and hot water, and it can become your chopping table once the cooking is done.

> NOTE: A friend asked me to help him cook a hog at his house. All he had was kosher salt. I guess good old table salt wasn't good enough for him. Anyway, it was 2:00 in the morning when we were salting the pig, so we went with it. Twelve hours later, the hog was nearly done. I was trying to finish it off, but the skin wouldn't get crisp. I added more coals directly under it, but instead of blistering up, the skin was burning. The kosher salt hadn't dissolved and seeped into the skin as the finer iodized salt would, and the skin hadn't dried out properly during the cook. Long story short, use cheap table salt, not some fancy chef's salt. You need less of it, and it's easier to find in the store.

If you built the fire in your burn barrel early enough, about 60 to 90 minutes out, you should have coals built up in the bottom of the burn barrel. Keep adding wood to keep the barrel full to the top. You're going to need a lot of coals.

Wearing heat-resistant gloves is a good idea here. Start adding shovelfuls of hot coals into the pit. These coals won't go directly under the hog, but instead will line the perimeter of the pit's interior along the concrete block walls. The technique I use is to stand at one end of the pit and reach the shovel-head full of coals across to the other end. Tilt the head of the shovel toward the block wall and pull the shovel slowly back toward yourself. Shake it a bit as you move the shovel, and the coals will fall down to the base of the wall. You'll need about two shovelfuls on each of the long sides, and one shovelful on each of the short sides to get the pit heated up.

Once the hog is on, and the coals have been placed, cover the pit with the sheet metal. Slide the grill thermometer into the hole drilled for it, and it will stay here during the entire cook. The target temperature will remain 250°F for the duration of the cook. When it dips down to 225°F or 230°F, add a shovelful of hot coals down each side.

Add the coals as quickly (and carefully) as you can. You're losing heat as soon as the lid comes off. The longer it's off, the slower the cook. If there's an audience, the cameras will come out when the lid comes off, and the shutter clicks will drown out the crackling of the coals. They'll all groan when it goes right back on, but they'll be happy that the pig actually gets cooked.

STEP 6.
FLIP THE HOG

The hog starts skin side up, but finishes skin side down. A flip is required in between. We used to wait until morning to flip our hogs at Skylight. By that time they were almost done and about to fall apart. It was a risky proposition that didn't make much sense in hindsight, but that's the way we'd always done it. Any morning could be ruined by a hog that fell apart. Valuable barbecue would drop into the pit, and a river of fat would drain into the fire from the cracked skin. The long and short of it is that our pork is more valuable on a plate than in the bottom of a pit.

About seven years ago, we started flipping the hogs the night before instead. The target internal temperature is around 130°F, which is usually after about 4 hours of cooking, which means the muscles are still tight. The hog isn't working so hard against you at that point, so at the restaurant, one person can flip hogs by himself.

A two-person team is best to flip the hog in your backyard. Both should stand on the same side of the pig, one at the shoulders and one at the hams. Wearing heat-resistant gloves that cover the forearms, slide the hog toward you, slowly, while you each reach underneath it with the hand closest to the center of the pit. Find the indentation at the fold of the spine and place your fingers there. Grab the leg closest to you with the other hand in preparation for flipping the hog over away from you. Count to three, and in one smooth motion, while lifting and pulling with the hand that's under the hog, flip it completely over. Slide it rather than picking it up and slamming it down. Make sure both people flip it together, or you'll end up with a whole hog bowtie. Once flipped, you should see a nice browning starting to develop on the skin. After admiring the hog, place the lid back on top of the pit.

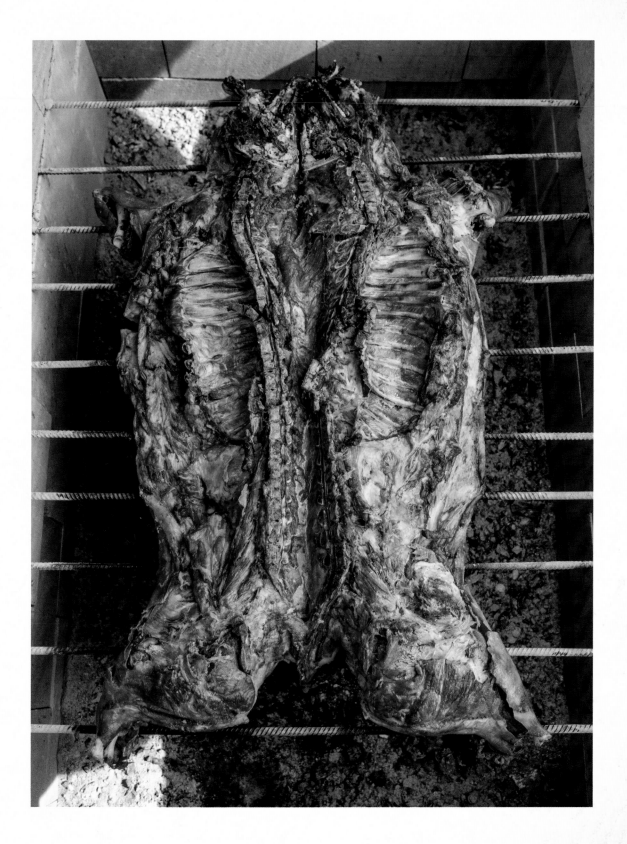

CHECK THE HOG'S INTERNAL TEMPERATURE

Keep a probe thermometer handy to check the meat temperature during the cook. I use a Thermapen MK4. It gives a quick, accurate reading, and it's waterproof. Take these readings at the shoulder or the ham portion.

90°F to 100°F
(approximately 3 to 4 hours into the cook)

This first reading is to ensure safety and to prevent spoiling. When it's cold out, there's a slight risk of the denser parts of the pig spoiling if you are cooking too slow. That may sound crazy, but I've witnessed it.

120°F to 130°F
(approximately 5 hours into the cook)

This is the point where you want to flip the hog. Any later, and it may be too tender to stay intact. You'll be hit with hog shrapnel, and good meat will fall to the ground.

160°F
(approximately 3 to 4 hours after the flip)

This is the target temperature. The hog isn't done yet at this point, but it's getting mighty close.

175°F
(anywhere from 10 to 12 hours into the cook)

This reading in the shoulders means the hog is done or close to done. Use it as a measurement, but not a final determination. One of the signs I look for are the ribs separating from the spine. This may happen first in the center of the hog. The closer this separation is toward the shoulders, the closer you are to the finish line.

It is possible to overcook a pig, especially if it's lean, but the whole hog cooking process is a forgiving one. Once the pig reaches 175°F internal, back the heat off in the pit to somewhere around 200°F. You can let the pig ride like this for hours until it's time to blister the skin. In fact, the longer it sits at this low pit temperature, the easier the skin will blister. Just don't let the internal temperature of the pig climb to the 200°F territory.

185°F

This is the target temperature in the shoulders and hams for the hog to be done. It should arrive at this temperature during the process of blistering the skin.

STEP 8.
CRISP THE SKIN

For God so loved the world, he gave us pork skins. Crispy skin is paramount to our barbecue style. It's what gives our barbecue its signature flavor, and it's why the cooking method has an extra level of difficulty. Cooking whole hog is easy until it comes to crisping the skin. This is the step where you can most easily ruin hours' worth of work.

The process really began when the skin of the raw hog was covered in salt. The salt wicks moisture away from the skin, so it can more easily get brown and crisp during the final step of the cook. The low, slow heat of the pit helps dry it out along the way, too. Dry hog skin blisters more readily than moist skin.

About 90 minutes before you want to serve the hog, it's time to start blistering the skin. Place a shovel of coals down each side of the pit and put the lid back on. This will bring the temperature of the pit up. Your pit will need to be at 275°F for the blistering to start. You'll soon see the smoke change from being some lazy plumes to pumping and churning smoke. There's some pressure building inside the pit because fat is dripping onto the coals. This is where the risk of fire is the greatest. Don't be afraid to lift that lid and check often. The last thing you want to do is burn that skin. It is the crowning jewel of this whole hog.

Once the pit is holding at 275°F, spread a few, and I mean a *few* coals—maybe a half-shovel's worth—directly under the pig. Place the lid back on and watch the pit temperature closely. The thermometer and volume of smoke are your tells as to whether a small flame-up is occurring.

I've cooked a pile of pigs, and there are some hogs where I just couldn't get the skin right no matter what I did. There are other hogs that were nearly done already when I fired the pit temperature back up.

Keep an eye on the skin as it blisters. The skin can burn as quickly as toast under a broiler or a marshmallow over a flame. Monitor it closely. Check it every 3 to 5 minutes. You can use the back of a knife to tap the skin to know when it begins to crisp. Scrape coals away from areas that start to burn. This process will only take about 20 to 30 minutes.

Once the blistering is done, the hog is ready to chop. If there are still hot coals directly under the hog, use the shovel to scrape them away toward the edges of the pit. If you need to hold off on serving for a bit, be sure not to let the pit cool too much, as this will allow the skin to soften again. Keeping the pit warm will actually make the skin even more crisp.

Figure 5. STAGES OF SKIN BROWNING AND BLISTERING

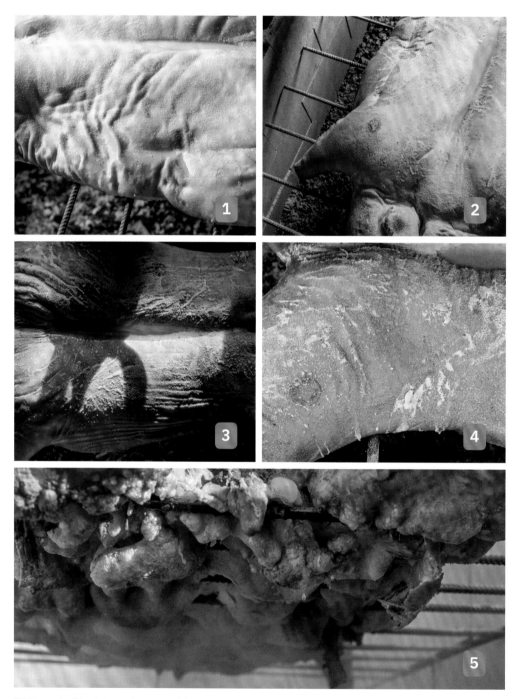

(1) Raw pigskin. (2) Two hours in. (3) Four hours in. (4) Five hours in. (5) Finished.

TIMELINE FOR A NOON WHOLE HOG PARTY

10:00 p.m.

Fire the pit and get it heated up to 250°F. Put the hog on.

3:00 a.m.

The hog should hit an internal temperature of 120°F to 130°F. Flip the hog, and add coals to bring the pit back up to 250°F to 275°F.

Four to five hours later, the internal temperature in the ham should be 160°F. From here you can coast to the finish line if you're ahead of schedule, or keep pushing it if necessary.

By 10:00 a.m., the internal temperature in the shoulder should be 180°F. The hog is done, but the skin is not.

10:30 a.m.

Check the skin for crispness. Add coals directly underneath the skin if necessary and watch the skin closely. Don't rush this part. At best you'll scorch the skin, and at worst you'll start a fire fueled by melted pig fat.

11:45 a.m.

Quarter the hog and bring it to the chopping block.

NOTE: For a 7:00 p.m., whole hog supper, slide the start time up seven hours and begin at 5:00 a.m.

At both Skylight Inn and Sam Jones BBQ, the time line is stretched out a bit. Hogs have a remarkable capability to hold on to their internal heat, so we let them ride overnight.

The hogs go on cold at roughly 34°F and are flipped at around 120°F. Coals are added to the pit as the daytime pit crew leaves Skylight at 8:00 p.m. If needed, another load of coals may go into the pits again around 11:00 p.m., then they coast until the crew gets back at 6:00 a.m. the next morning. The Sam Jones pit house runs a little later because we open later there. But, it's only a few hours of difference in timing. The processes are identical.

Pit staff will check the hogs to see which one is further along. That hog will be first to start the process of blistering the skin so it's ready at 10:00 a.m. when the doors open at Skylight.

CHOP THE MEAT

Remember, in eastern North Carolina, we don't eat our pork pulled. We chop it. The ingredients for our chopped barbecue are simple, but don't go thinking it's just pork and vinegar. The pork has to have the right ratio of lean meat, fatty meat, and crispy skin. At the restaurants, we chop one-quarter of the hog at a time. Rib meat, belly meat, loin, and hams will all get chopped together, so the dry meat from the ham can soak up the extra fat from the belly.

Set up a table near the pit that can be used as a chopping table. Place a large cutting board on the table, and at least one meat cleaver for chopping. Place some damp towels under the cutting block if you'd like. It will keep it from sliding on the table.

Back in the pit, with a knife, cut the hog in half right down the middle of the spine. This will be a little challenging where the skin touches the rods. Then, cut one of the halves in half, between the tenth and eleventh ribs, starting your count from the front of the pig. This will allow easy transport from pit to cutting board. (Or, if you're feeling flashy and confident, enlist several friends to help you carry the whole thing.) With the heat-resistant gloves on, lift one quarter of the hog into a large tub, hotel pan, or sheet tray, and take it to the chopping table. Leave the remaining three quarters of the hog in the pit, and replace the lid.

Now the bones, cartilage, and gristle need to be removed and tossed. Scoop the meat that remains out of the skin and onto a large cutting block. Continue to look for pieces of bone and gristle to pull out. Once all the meat is on the cutting board, it's time to evaluate the skin.

Not all the skin can be chopped into the barbecue. Some of the skin, like what you find on the hocks or at the top of the legs, is leathery and needs to be thrown out. The skin that's brittle enough to crack when you bend it is the stuff to look for. Think toffee texture instead of jerky. Chop whatever skin you deem worth eating into bits. Always chop the skin first. This will allow the meat to stay hotter longer. The meat cools rapidly once chopped, and you'll be adding liquid seasoning to it, which will cool it further. Add skin to the meat that's waiting to be chopped.

Two meat cleavers working together are the preferred tools for the job, but one works fine too. Once the meat mixture has been tamed into a manageable mound (but not quite completely chopped), it's time to add the seasoning.

SEASON THE MEAT

You may have heard some slander against whole hog barbecue saying that it all tastes like vinegar. Sure we use vinegar, but a restrained amount. We want to add some acidity to the meat, but you've still got to taste the pork and the smoke. The barbecue that's so packed with vinegar it'll clear your sinuses—that stuff is from joints that cook with gas and have no wood smoke. They need to provide some other flavor to the pork. They do it with loads of sauce.

At Skylight Inn, the ingredients in the seasoning are applied separately. Salt and black pepper cascade down from shakers held high above the chopped pork. Rivers of hot sauce and vinegar flow from bottles and splash onto the barbecue. It's mesmerizing to watch, like seeing an artist in action. There's a mystique that comes along with seeing this inexact science at work on top of the barbecue, which itself is the result of an inexact cooking process. It takes training to get the quantities and proportions right.

At Sam Jones BBQ, we had the challenge of a much larger staff who did not have the years of experience of the Skylight crew. If we let them all season things their own way, we'd have some issues with consistency, so we started mixing the sauce in its correct proportions.

The ingredient quantities listed on page 62 are for about 70 pounds of servable meat, which is what you should end up with from a 180-pound hog, assuming the skin is properly blistered and added to the meat. The proper ratio is ¼ cup of sauce to 1 pound of meat. Measure out the sauce, add it to the meat, and chop it a little more to mix it all in.

If you'd like more hot sauce, or you can't ever get enough salt, feel free to sprinkle either on separately to your liking. Remember, you can always add more, but you can't take it out. Place that seasoned meat in a large pan for serving. It's party time.

Return to the pit to fetch another quarter of the hog, and bring it to the chopping block to repeat the process. Hopefully the first quarter of the pig is gone, and it's time for a refill of the serving pan. Chop the remaining quarters of the pig as needed to keep the crowd fed.

If everyone you invited comes, you may end up eating the whole hog. If not, there are several ways to handle the leftovers.

Chop and season all the remaining meat, and let folks carry some home. If folks are gathered around the chopping table, but full of pork, cut

the skin up in chip-size pieces because they'll all find room for another bite of skin. Besides, the skin won't be this crunchy in tomorrow's leftovers. Whatever you take home with you will make good cold sandwiches, or it can be repurposed for a stew.

Once all the meat has been chopped and served, if they haven't already been lured in by the intoxicating smell that has filled the area, invite all the neighborhood dogs over to clean up the ground around the chopping table.

NOTE: The dogs may never leave.

Three

SAM JONES BBQ

Third-Generation Perfection

I never thought I'd own my own barbecue restaurant. Heck, at one point in my life I decided to quit barbecue for good. I was working at Skylight during my teenage years with both Pete and Bruce. Each of them can be gruff, but Bruce raised me to always be respectful, and he never let anyone be disrespectful, or embarrass me in front of anyone. One day I did something wrong, but it wasn't anything big. It didn't matter to Pete. At the counter, in the middle of a full restaurant, Pete just laid into me. He wasn't used to being talked back to, but I wheeled around and said, "Who do you think you're talking to?" I lost it. His jaw dropped when I told him, "I ain't one of your hunting dogs, you understand? Just because I'm your grandson, doesn't mean I have to work here. Do you get that?" I didn't pursue another career the next day or anything, but I never forgot that day. I don't think he did, either.

I went to work for one of my dad's former business partners at age fifteen. The gun shop was a lot cooler than the barbecue place. Glenn Bowen, who was also a good friend of my granddad Jones, let me come on board. I worked there through the rest of high school. Then, reluctantly, I left for college.

It was in college of all places that I came to understand the importance of the family business. I was given a writing assignment, fifteen pages about any subject I wanted. Thinking it would be almost unfairly easy, I chose barbecue. It started with this long family barbecue legacy in Ayden, the stories I had heard in my youth, my granddaddy, my dad, and my former place of employment. Except when looking back, Skylight didn't seem like it had just been a job anymore. Barbecue was more than how we made a living. Cooking whole hog barbecue was part of the Joneses' identity. When I turned that paper in, I realized it could be up to me to take the torch and keep the coals lit.

While still in college, I went back to working part time at Skylight. I came in one afternoon in 2003, and Pete told me a woman from New York had called, and he told her that I would call her back. That was the first 212 area code I had ever dialed on purpose. She said she was from the James Beard Foundation. Back then, that meant nothing to me, but I listened. She said we would be receiving a James Beard award in the America's Classics category at a ceremony in New York, and she'd like the family to come accept the award.

The first thing I said was, "How much is this going to cost?" She laughed. I didn't, and I explained, "Ma'am, I'm really not trying to be funny. I'm asking because I know that's what I'll be asked." She estimated about $1,200. I hung the phone up in the storage room and walked through the kitchen to the front counter. On one end of the counter was Pete, Bruce on the other, and uncle Jeff at the chopping block. Pete and Bruce were in one of their funks where they'd go a month or so without speaking. I repeated what I'd been told, that it was the Oscars of the food world, and asked Pete and Bruce if they wanted to go. Pete said, "I don't wanna go. Bruce, do you want to go?" Bruce, without even looking at us, said, "No," like somebody had just asked him if he wanted a colonoscopy. Pete looked at Jeff and he shook his head. Then Pete asked if I wanted to go. "Heck yeah, I want to go."

It wasn't so much about getting the award, but I'd never been to New York. The flight was only $119, and I asked all my friends if anybody wanted to go. No takers. I went a few days before the awards and did all the touristy things. I went and saw the Statue of Liberty and the Empire State building, and visited several fire stations, as well the NYC fire museum.

On Monday, I arrived at the awards in my black tuxedo and sat down in the auditorium looking just like I knew what all this was about. Before long they took me backstage. I thought, "This is like the country music awards. This is a big deal." I went on stage when they called me up. R. W. Apple Jr., a distinguished food writer I have since learned, put the medal around my neck, and I don't even remember if I said anything.

I went up to the reception area, and all they had was wine and water. I didn't care for either, so I went snooping around to find a Coke. I was sitting just outside the reception area drinking a Coke with a medal around my neck. At this point I'd been in New York for two days, and not a single person wanted to talk to me, or cared who I was. Now, all at once, this medal is hanging around my neck, and everyone wanted to get to know me. This lady came up and asked me a question, to which I responded,

"Yes, ma'am." She must have liked my accent because she asked me to say it again, then asked if I wanted to go an after-party. We went from one place to the next, and I didn't get back to my room until five in the morning.

Until last year, the medal has been on display at Skylight. The funny thing is, fifteen years after getting an award, the significance of which we barely understood, the Atlanta History Center has it on display in their Barbecue Nation exhibition.

It wasn't long after the James Beard awards that granddad's health went downhill for good. I took off a semester to return full time to the family business. My newfound faith in barbecue didn't make the job any easier, but it allowed me to see my place within a larger scheme. I never got another semester of school under my belt.

I thought being on that stage in New York City, getting a medal put around my neck, was the pinnacle when it came to accolades for my barbecue career, so it hit me like a hammer right between the eyes when I saw my name as a James Beard Foundation semifinalist for Best Chef Southeast in 2018. I say that because my eyes produced tears as I stared at my name on a list among friends and chefs I greatly admire. Not in a million years did I expect it. I still don't consider myself in that class. Historically, barbecue cooks haven't been represented in those awards. Until its somewhat recent popularity, barbecue was in the basement of the food chain. I think that's because barbecue, historically, was a food created by, and for, the poor. For a long time it was viewed as peasant food that doesn't require much skill to prepare.

What's crazier is to think that sort of recognition could come just three years after opening Sam Jones BBQ. It was hard to fathom. It really validated my decision to branch out in my own direction, a decision that seemed crazy at first.

I've been called the owner of Skylight Inn in more food magazine stories than I can count, but I've never owned even 1 percent of the family business. Skylight Inn belongs to my dad and Uncle Jeff. I've always been proud to be a part of the business, where I still am the decision maker and have been treated as a partner for years, but I wanted something to own, something that was mine. Mainly, something that would provide security, as I would be in control of a succession plan that my family never had. Opening Sam Jones BBQ was a way to have control over the decisions that led to success, or didn't.

Yet I would not have had the personal or professional confidence to open my own place without a little emotional encouragement—and a push—from a few people on the outside. One was John T. Edge. Most anyone reading should know who John T. is, but for those who don't, he is an accomplished writer and directs the Southern Foodways Alliance. In 2009, during Skylight's lean years, the SFA shot a short film, *Capital Q*, about us and invited me to the Big Apple BBQ Block Party for a question-and-answer segment after the film. I remember walking around that festival staring at folks who now are some of my greatest friends. I looked at them like they were rock stars. Sure, we'd been cooking hogs for a whole lot of years, but I still couldn't piece together how I'd arrived on this grand stage. I was really pumped when they invited me back the following year to do a small event associated with the Block Party and to serve our barbecue.

Fast-forward a bit to 2010, when I first met Nick Pihakis, cofounder of Jim 'N Nick's BBQ based in Birmingham, Alabama—another friend I credit with giving me the push I needed to open my own place. Now, I've shared my barbecue in New York, Chicago, Hawaii, Sweden, and all points in between, but back then, the whole idea of traveling outside Ayden for barbecue events was new to me. The first event I did was an SFA dinner at Charleston Wine + Food, which is where I first met Nick. The SFA asked me to come be a part of it. I did not want to do it. One, I saw no value in it. Two, it was completely out of my comfort zone. We lived in the four walls of that restaurant all those years.

John T. had called, explained what they wanted to do, and asked if I would do it. "Oh yeah, man. I can help you with that," I told him—with the full intention of not going. I didn't even make a note or write down the date. Then Nick Pihakis called me. "Hey, just touching base . . ." I continued to put these guys off. Nick finally gave it one more shot. "Hey man, are you going to do this, or not?" He understood the importance of the SFA, and wanted our family to get recognition for their work more than I did. I made up everything I could think of. Finally, I said, "Mr. Pihakis, it's one thing for you to think I'm a fool and for me stay here in Ayden, North Carolina. It's a whole different thing for me to drive to Charleston and prove you right in front of a lot of people." He busted out laughing and said, "Just bring your ass down here. I know you'll do fine." I reluctantly agreed.

When I got to Charleston, we met at the Jim 'N Nick's location on King Street, right in the heart of the town. Pat Martin was the only person in attendance I knew, and I didn't know him well. John Haire, the local owner there at the time, made me feel super welcome. Fellow whole hog pitmaster Rodney Scott, who was in the same rookie position I was just a year before, met me at 3:30 that morning, and that's how our friendship kicked off.

The event came off great. Just before the barbecue was served, the festival showed the short film *Capital Q.* As we marched through the front door hoisting a whole hog on a tray, real high-class people in my book stood to their feet and applauded. I was thinking, "Man, this is so odd." We've been cooking hogs a long time to zero applause.

I remember calling my dad at the end of the event in Charleston. I said, "There's something to this. I don't know exactly what, but there's an outside world that really cares about what we're doing." He was stubborn, and of the mind-set that my grandfather would have been: if you're not inside these four walls, you're not being productive for the company. I might as well have been on a fishing trip in his mind. As more opportunities for travel and barbecue festivals came up, we had some head-butting competitions about doing all these events and me being gone so much. Bruce didn't seem to understand that our restaurant was getting busier as a result.

Even now, some of the locals don't understand. "Why do you travel all over the country?" they ask. "Them people aren't coming to buy no barbecue from you." They're just like I used to be. But if I hadn't taken a chance in Charleston, I wouldn't have met so many people who are now close friends, nor would I have become part of the FatBack Collective—a group of chefs, writers, and barbecue folk. I'm not one to name-drop, but I do like bragging on my friends. The FatBack ranks include some of the brightest minds and kindest folks I've ever had the pleasure of being associated with: Nick, John T., Pat Martin, Sean Brock, Ryan Prewitt, Donald Link, Ashley Christensen, Rodney Scott, Drew Robinson, Wright Thompson, and Stephen Stryjewski, just to name a few. To be included in this company years ago was such an honor to me.

In May 2011, the FatBack Collective entered the World Championship Barbecue Cooking Contest in Memphis and took third place in whole hog, which was pretty nuts given none of us had a knowledge of competition barbecue. Not knowing any better, we did it with a Mangalitsa hog, wood-fired, with no injection. Mangalitsa is a breed that costs a fortune because the pigs have so much fat, and there weren't a lot of them in the US at the time. I'll tell you, I learned that those hogs are not intended for making barbecue. They're intended for making sausage, or a big fire in your pit. (You see, the fattier a hog breed, the more likely that fat, once it melts, will crest the edges of the carcass. That means hot, liquid fat, aka "pig napalm," will flow directly into the coals below and start a fire big enough to be seen the next county over.) Still, it was an honor to take third place doing it the way we wanted to. Pure.

Then, 2013 was my first invitation to go to New York for the Big Apple Barbecue Block Party. Kenny Callaghan, at the time the chef and pitmaster at the Manhattan barbecue restaurant Blue Smoke, called and invited me.

All I knew is that I didn't want to go up there and look like a basketball team that never practiced. I told him, "Well, Kenny, all I need to know is what it takes to be there." It boiled down to being able to handle the volume: about three thousand portions per day. He said, "Let's just say ten hogs. If you can do ten hogs a day, consider yourself officially invited." I told him that I planned to hit the ground running as soon as we hung up the phone. What I didn't say is that I didn't actually have a rig to facilitate such an event.

You see, the first time I ever visited the Big Apple Barbecue was as a spectator, back in 2008. At a bar called the Black Bear, which hosted the unofficial pitmaster after-party (often referred to as the "Kenny Callaghan Invitational"), at about three in the morning, I launched into an argument, or rather a debate, with Nashville pitmasters Pat Martin and Carey Bringle, aka Peg Leg Porker. I was green as a gourd, and I was sitting there talking to these guys who were very welcoming to me. Pat said, "Sam, would you ever do this event?" My response verbatim was, "Man, this just blows my mind to even think about how I could do this."

Being ignorant as I was, I said, "I just couldn't see me being able to do it without bringing a bunch of cinder blocks up here." Pat and Carey looked at me as if I were wearing a bear's head for a hat. Pat said, "Look here, Captain, you're just not going to bring an eighteen-wheeler of cinder blocks and dump them on Madison Avenue and start you a fire. That just ain't gonna work." Pat continued, "Well, you know, you can do it, but you got to make some concessions to pull something like this off."

My wife, Sarah, was sitting there with all of us like, "Really, it's three in the morning. You're talking about something hypothetical at this point." For those who don't know Pat, Carey, or me, imagine three strong-headed but like-minded guys from the South debating how you should cook hogs on a New York City street. I finally, ever so kindly, said, "Screw it, then. Maybe I won't do this event." It's funny to reflect on because Carey Bringle told me he came away from the bar thinking, "Man, this guy's stupid and an asshole to boot." Pat simply said, "Let me know how all them blocks work out for you." The funny thing is Carey, Pat, and I have been great friends ever since. It did make me realize that how stupid you are depends on what you're talking about.

I remembered my conversation with Pat and Carey in 2013, when I agreed to go up there to cook. I wanted to make sure that we had a good showing. You're not just representing your brand—you're representing your food group, your style of barbecue. In my opinion, I was there for all of eastern North Carolina. I was an ambassador. That's a lot to hang your cap on. The last thing I wanted to do was go up there and fumble the ball.

After I hung up with Kenny that day, we began having our big rig built. The "Big Rig" is a thirty-six-foot-long gooseneck trailer wielding eight wood-fired whole hog cookers on it in the design of the first cooker BQ Grills built for me. When Pat saw it, in true Pat Martin fashion, he said, "This sure beats the hell out of an eighteen-wheeler load of cinder blocks, don't it?" We both had a good laugh at that one.

Events like the James Beard Awards, the Big Apple Barbecue, and that first SFA dinner at Charleston Wine + Food are how I became the face, or mouthpiece, of Skylight Inn outside the Ayden area. We were able to reach a wider audience than ever before. Just being able to serve our barbecue next to the barbecue titans at Big Apple elevated our reputation.

Somewhere deep down I always wanted to do something to further the family business. I didn't know how, nor did I have a family that did. In their minds, we should just do what Pete did and be happy with the result. Though I had been treated as a financial partner at Skylight, I didn't have the security of a formal, full partnership. Then something big changed in my life: I was a new daddy. I needed security for that little girl. I'm a firm believer in the saying "Do as you've always done, and get what you've always got."

Sitting in a hotel in Somewhere, USA, my friend Nick Pihakis said, "You need your own place, and I'll help you." In a subsequent conversation he said, "You know you'll need a partner if you open a place." Now you would think he was referring to himself, but he wasn't. He continued by saying, "You'll need someone you trust to have your back and to operate the home front for you when you're on the road." His exact words: "You need someone to give a shit like you give a shit." Nick compared the opening of a restaurant to an album being made. Once the album is done and spinning, you have to return to the road to promote it. Opening and running a restaurant while also going on "tour" isn't something I could do alone.

Nick said, "You're going to need someone to be in your corner." When he said that, the person that kept coming up in my head was Michael Letchworth.

You've got those people who are as close to you as family, maybe even more so. One afternoon when I was twenty-one years old, Jason Worley, one of my best friends, and I were sitting on ATVs on the canal bank on the backside of the farm I grew up on. We had stopped to smoke a cigarette when this kid, Michael Letchworth, rode up on a four-wheeler nicer than ours. We got to chatting a bit, and he said he lived up the road. After learning he was only fourteen, I asked who his dad was. I then realized I had known his family my whole life. His dad was the funeral director for Farmer Funeral Service in Ayden. The same guy who carried my dad to the hospital when he was basically lifeless was the guy Michael's dad apprenticed under.

Michael was that guy I could count on. I knew it when he started working at Skylight. When it came time to do something, Michael was the general to lead the charge. That's his personality. It could be opening a

Me and Michael Letchworth.

restaurant, or drilling a tunnel through a mountain. He always finds a way. He was the only person I called. I didn't have a Plan B. If I needed a partner, that's the only person I wanted it to be. Michael wasn't so sure about it, as he tells it:

Samuel was invited to compete on the television show *BBQ Pitmasters* in the fall of 2012. He called a local guy, Billy Merril, who had done competitions in the past, to come and help. One of the other contestants on the show put together a charity event in Raleigh that was going to include everyone that was on the show. He needed an extra set of hands, and there wasn't anybody extra from Skylight to go, so I went to help. I had spent plenty of time working at Skylight, but I had never cooked a pig. I hadn't even carried a shovel of coals at that time. The only reason I'd go to the cookhouse was to get a quarter pig off the pit to chop.

We cooked a pig for the charity event. It was the first time I was able to be a part of the process start to finish. I chopped it, Samuel and Billy served it, and everybody seemed to like it. There were a few other barbecue joints there, and when the judges announced the people's choice prize, we won. I felt some pride, and it started to make sense. For the first time, I quit taking everything Skylight did for granted.

It wasn't long after that Samuel asked me if he opened his own place, would I have any interest in coming to work there, and possibly managing it? I told him yes. I never expected him to call me, but a few months later, he did, and offered me to be his partner in this new place. My thought was, "How is this going to happen?" I didn't have any money. I was twenty-six with just enough to pay the bills and keep cold beer in the fridge. I wasn't sure how it was going to work, and I was nervous to ask Samuel, but I said "yes" anyway. The next spring, we were setting up for a festival in Farmville, and he says we need to plan a visit to the bank. "You're gonna be signing the loan right along with me," he said, and I gulped. "Will they even finance this with my name on it?"

They did give us a loan, and we both signed it in late 2014. Neither of us really knew what it was going to take to open our own restaurant. I was thirty-three at the time and Michael was twenty-six. Michael is a details guy, and I didn't have a whole lot of details to give him. It was a lot of blind faith and trust. It got more serious quickly. I hired an architect from Colorado, which came with a $120,000 commitment. Every day was an emotional roller coaster. Some mornings I thought we'd just kill it over there, and other mornings I was thinking, "What have you done?" I knew what was on the line. In January 2015, our contractor backed out, and we basically went through a divorce with our architect. I had risked everything I'd worked for the first thirty-four years of my life. I had put it all on the line for collateral.

At the rate we were spending, it wasn't going to take long to eat up my finances. There was a $25,000 bill for our branding. Nick, Michael, and I would talk once a week about the progress, and I would question something like that. Nick would assure me. "Trust it," he would say. "What you're trying to do is build a brand, and you aren't gonna do that with just a sign by the road."

I sought a partnership with my dad and Jeff, but they weren't interested. They were comfortable with their ownership stake in Skylight Inn and weren't looking to rock the boat so late in life. I felt like I was giving up conquered ground by not calling it Skylight Inn. Heck, at one point, the floor plan for the new building was a hexagon, just like Skylight, but we knew that this new restaurant was a chance to create a breath of fresh air. We scrapped that design pretty quickly and decided to make a statement about our vision of what eastern North Carolina barbecue could be. We needed a restaurant and a menu that made a profit while highlighting our very centerpiece of whole hog barbecue. One thing we never questioned were the words of Pete Jones:

"If it's not cooked with wood it's not BBQ."

I don't say it quite like he did because that is a very bold statement. However, gas cookers have become prevalent at barbecue joints in North Carolina and beyond, but remaining true to our barbecue roots, whole hog barbecue cooked over wood is the backbone of Sam Jones BBQ. No matter that hog cooking is the most financially irresponsible thing you can do. The time required to cook an entire pig that you can only serve a little more than a third of and the effort required to make sure fresh barbecue comes off the pit throughout the day make us even question if we're sane. Add in the barrier that folks in our area aren't used to paying what you need to charge for it. People in eastern North Carolina don't think whole hog is that special, well, until their favorite joint closes up shop. It's commonplace

because it's a part of life around here. Some out-of-town food writer might be all excited about the idea and the aesthetics of whole hog cooked over wood, but the folks here are like, "Well, your pork per pound better not be more than $13." So, you still wanna cook barbecue for a living? Great idea.

We knew we had to expand the menu if we were going to pay the bills. We knew the market in the Greenville area would likely demand more options than pork in a tray or pork in a sandwich. Michael had some success with ribs and turkey, and less with brisket, on a pit he'd built in his backyard. We added more sides and desserts too. But nothing would be more controversial than adding a few taps for cold beer.

By the time opening day rolled around, on November 10, 2015, so much work and energy had already gone into the restaurant. We had all these projections and expectations wrapped up in this day. Everybody was gathered. We had thirty-seven employees to handle the counter, the bar, the barbecue, and the rest of the cooking, which was more than I'd ever managed, and certainly more than Michael ever had. It was fifteen minutes until opening, and I asked Michael to step into the storage room. I said, "I want you to know that I love you, and whatever comes from here, we're going to do it together." We both started crying. We said a word of prayer, dried our eyes, and walked back out to the front.

I went out to unlock the front door, and there were people everywhere. Cars were wrapped around the building waiting for the drive-thru, and customers were lined up waiting for that door to open. We hadn't advertised, so it was a relief because at least people were here, but we knew we weren't going to be able to ease into it. Thankfully there were people to help us on opening day. Nick Pihakis, his son Nicholas, his daughter Catherine, and Leigh Ledbetter helped us train our staff. We had the likes of Billy Durney and Rodney Scott, who had come to volunteer. Pat Martin was expediting food, and Angie Mosier sat cross-legged on the sidewalk outside of the building and torched plywood to mount the photos that hang inside the restaurant. Like the rest of them, she never sent me a bill. So many from our barbecue family came to help.

We opened at 11:00 a.m., and even with all the help, we closed at 3:00 p.m. Nick was there and said, "You need to shut this down and regroup." It was shaky. It was like pulling a trailer that was loaded improperly. You know, when you get the trailer up to speed, it shakes violently, and the only way to fix it is to slow down. We had loaded our trailer improperly, and it shook violently for four hours. There was no way we were going to get it under control unless we stopped for a while.

For two hours, somebody had to stand at the door and tell people we were closed. It was a bit of a morale crusher, but dinner went a little better. We made it until 8:15 p.m., less than an hour shy of the planned closing time.

For weeks there were people lined up at the door when we opened. Twenty cars would be in the drive-thru. Michael and I were miserable. Because of volume and lack of staff, we were tag-teaming in and out. I would stay late and make sure the hogs were getting up to temperature, and Michael would come in early. There was a time, for the first few months, that there weren't but two or three hours in the day when one of us wasn't in the building. Take it from Michael:

I worked ninety days straight. The first thirty of those days were almost twenty hours a day. I could have never imagined something that could be so rewarding and just as draining as opening a new restaurant. It was like being thrown in the deep end. Some people think this is some golden ticket to the easy life. They don't see the sacrifices you make personally, and the sacrifices your family makes.

Even I questioned my decision. I came home one night and lay down in bed at quarter 'til two, smelling like pig smoke. I didn't even take a shower because I had to be back there at 6:30 a.m. I was staring at the ceiling, and Sarah asked, "Are you all right?" I was as exhausted as I could be, and I said, "Honest to God, I'm asking myself what I have done, because if this is how life is going to be from here on out, I don't want any part of it."

A restaurant is a lot like a microphone. You don't get anything out of it that you don't put in it. We were putting plenty in, but thankfully that was the bottom of the roller coaster. By the end of 2016, things leveled out, and it all felt right.

When we first opened, there were so many rumors that my dad and I were angry at one another, or there had been a falling-out in the family. That's why they thought I got my own place. There were even some in my own family who had not-so-nice things to say. To battle that perception, the first month I had Mike "Chopper" Parrott chopping here on loan from the chopping block at Skylight. Uncle Jeff was out front bussing tables. I didn't want anyone saying that the barbecue was different over here, and I wanted to clear up the idea of a family quarrel.

There was, however, that disagreement about beer. My dad is a Baptist preacher and doesn't drink a drop. Neither he nor my mother was happy when they learned we'd be serving beer, along with being open on Sundays. He told a friend of mine, "I'm still proud of Samuel. I'm just disappointed in that area." Plenty of locals were, too. There's a "bless your heart" section in the Greenville paper. My guess is, it was intended for people to share good deeds or favors that other folks, maybe strangers, had done for them. Things like, "Thanks to the young man who helped carry groceries to my car." Stuff like that. Unfortunately, some people use it for the bad. One person wrote in to say, "Bless your heart to all the barbecue restaurants in the area that aren't serving beer." It wasn't very welcoming, nor a morale booster by any stretch.

Other rumors hurt me even more: that we weren't cooking with wood or weren't really cooking whole hogs. I had a good mind to put up a sign on the smokehouse out here that said "Ayden," because everybody just said, "Well, you know they're just cooking everything in Ayden."

We cook the whole hogs at Sam Jones BBQ the same as we cook them at Skylight. We think they taste just as good as the original, but some understandably have their doubts. That included my dad when he finally visited. Because of the beer, he didn't grace the restaurant for three months after we opened.

We don't serve leftover barbecue, so we throw away the last of the chopped pork at the end of the night at both restaurants, but Skylight closes two hours before Sam Jones BBQ. If there's anything left, they bring it ten minutes up the road to our restaurant to chop and serve. That barbecue is still fresh when it gets here.

Well, Bruce didn't know this the first time he came in for dinner around 8:00 p.m. He ordered barbecue and baked beans. I went over to the table he and mom were seated at because I knew something wasn't going to be right. That's just the Jones way. I asked him what he thought. He said, "It's pretty good, but this barbecue is a little different." As soon as he said that, I would've turned my back on $1,000 to keep that comment. I strung him along and asked him what was different. He said, "I know it's cooked the same. Maybe it's not seasoned the same." I laughed and asked him, "What would you say if I told you that came from your place?" His response—"I stand corrected"—was some kind of good to me.

He had no idea what we were doing. For me, I knew the barbecue was going to be the part folks pointed to when they wanted to create some sort of gap between what we were cooking and what Skylight was cooking. I just didn't think my own pappy would fall victim to it.

Skylight is the original. We get that. To some people, we'll never be able to match it. To some, Sam Jones BBQ will always be the stepchild to Pete Jones's place. To others, it's the opposite. But we can't worry about that. We can only focus on the customers who choose to come try our whole hog barbecue, or anything else on the menu. We feel like ours is some of the best whole hog barbecue in the country because we don't cut any corners. As long as we're doing it the right way, that's enough for us.

RUB POTION NUMBER SWINE

Makes 3¹/2 cups

We've done whole hog all our lives. It doesn't take much more seasoning than salt and a little sauce at the end. Barbecue rubs were never something we had lying around the kitchen. When we opened Sam Jones BBQ, we were cooking things besides the whole hogs we'd done at Skylight. We added spare ribs, turkey breast, and chicken, and we needed a barbecue rub to season them. I'll let Michael Letchworth explain how he developed the one we use today. He calls it Rub Potion Number Swine:

> I was playing around on a new pit I'd built in the backyard, cooking ribs and chicken. I was spending a fortune on commercial rubs at the grocery store, so I asked my friend, Reid McMillan, for a rub recipe. His was kinda hot, and it had more stuff in it than I had at home. I'd never tasted celery salt. I pulled all the stuff out of my cabinet that qualified for a rub. I started writing down the mixtures and cooking with it. I would tweak it, and friends would give me comments until I dialed it in.
>
> I didn't really know what I was doing at the beginning. The first recipe had both garlic salt and garlic powder. It also had both onion powder and minced onion. I made a few changes, then bottled it for a Christmas gift in 2012. I needed a funny name for the label, so I called it Rub Potion Number Swine. I had a company bottle it in Memphis and I started selling it locally. When we were developing recipes for Sam Jones BBQ, Samuel asked if we could just use my rub recipe. Now it goes on just about everything, even the burgers.

There's a bottling company here in Ayden that makes our rub for us. You can purchase it on our website if you'd rather get the finished product.

1 cup paprika
1 cup light brown sugar
½ cup salt
¼ cup ground black pepper
¼ cup garlic powder
¼ cup ground mustard
¼ cup chili powder
1 tablespoon onion powder
2 tablespoons cayenne pepper

In a bowl, mix all the ingredients together well with a whisk or with gloved hands. Toss generously on any barbecue you cook, except the whole hog. Any remaining rub can be stored in a sealed container in a cool, dry place for several months.

SWEET BARBECUE SAUCE, AKA "BEAN SAUCE"

Makes 6 cups

The bean recipe we always made for catering at Skylight events required us to make a "bean sauce." It wasn't much more than a simple, sweet barbecue sauce, but batch after batch, we'd mix up the bean sauce from a half-dozen ingredients. When we opened Sam Jones BBQ, Michael and I developed a sweet barbecue sauce. We also use it on the ribs. The finished product in the bottle was pretty dang close to the bean sauce in flavor, sweetness, and consistency. That's why we don't make "bean sauce" at SJB anymore and instead use our bottled sweet sauce.

If you don't have any Sam Jones BBQ sweet sauce at home, you can always order some, or make the bean sauce recipe here. My dad still insists the beans are better with the bean sauce—something about heartburn—but it's not much different. I never have gotten an explanation as to why they add just a smidge of Kraft brand barbecue sauce at the end. Maybe it's a heartburn cure or something. Most likely, it's just because that's the way the Joneses always did it.

1¼ cups granulated sugar

1¼ cups light brown sugar

2 cups ketchup

2 tablespoons Worcestershire sauce

2 tablespoons yellow mustard

¼ cup Kraft barbecue sauce (I know, right?)

There's no need to heat this sauce. In a large bowl, combine all the ingredients and mix until the sugars are well dissolved. It will keep in the refrigerator for weeks.

EASTERN NORTH CAROLINA BARBECUE SAUCE

Makes about 1 quart

We have both a sweet barbecue sauce and a vinegar sauce that we bottle. The vinegar sauce is not the same vinegar mixture we pour over the hogs as they're chopped, but some folks like to pour a little on their barbecue sandwiches whether or not we think they need to. That's why we refer to it at the restaurant as "table sauce."

I liken this style of sauce more to a dressing than a sauce. It is thin, and shouldn't be overapplied. A straightforward, simple, vinegar-based sauce elevates the natural flavor of pork. Some sort of magical thing takes place with the acidity in the vinegar and the natural fat in hogs.

3 cups apple cider vinegar

½ cup sugar

2 tablespoons crushed red pepper

2 tablespoons ground black pepper

1 tablespoon chili powder

⅓ cup Texas Pete Hot Sauce

½ cup bottled barbecue sauce, such as Sweet Barbecue Sauce (page 128)

In a large bowl, combine all the ingredients and mix until the sugar is well dissolved. Alternatively, place in a jar with a tight-fitting lid and shake vigorously until the ingredients are combined.

FOR A WHOLE HOG PARTY
Makes about 1 gallon

3 quarts apple cider vinegar

2¼ cups sugar

½ cup crushed red pepper

½ cup ground black pepper

¼ cup chili powder

1½ cups Texas Pete Hot Sauce

2 cups bottled barbecue sauce, such as Sweet Barbecue Sauce (page 128)

The easiest way to mix a batch this size is to buy a gallon jug of apple cider vinegar. Remove one quart from the bottle, then, using a funnel, pour all the remaining ingredients into the jug. Close the lid tightly and shake the jug vigorously to combine.

PORK SPARE RIBS

Makes 3 to 4 servings

We bought a wood-fired cabinet smoker just for ribs because we couldn't keep up with demand when we first opened. The smoker is a big metal box fueled by wood chunks, but it's not really appropriate for home cooks due to its size and hefty price tag. It was the first barbecue-cooking implement we'd ever used that wasn't fueled solely by hardwood coals. After a few months of tweaking temperature settings and which racks the ribs should sit on, we gave up the fight. The results just weren't right. The ribs were either undercooked or too smoky, and we didn't have the time or help to figure it out.

One of our pit guys reverted back to cooking the ribs inside the whole hog pits during his shifts. We liked the flavor and made what in hindsight was an obvious change in methods. There's nothing that isn't improved by a little extra smoke from hog fat.

We brine the meat overnight, then rub it in the morning. The brine isn't necessary at home, but it helps with making consistently juicy ribs at the restaurant. The rub is best applied right before you put the slabs on the pit.

Feel free to season ribs as heavy or light as you like at home. At the restaurant, we evenly coat them from a shaker full of Rub Potion Number Swine (page 127). "Evenly coat" means a lot of different things to different people, but it's not a rub. The racks aren't dunked into a large pan full of rub, either. It's shaken on to a thickness where you can still see some of the meat underneath.

NOTE: The foil wrapping helps tenderize the ribs, and it also buys you some time. If you're at home executing an entire meal, it's hard to keep a close eye on meats that are cooking over direct heat. They might be burning while you're brewing sweet tea or mixing up the potato salad. The foil wrapper helps prevent that.

Brine
1 gallon water
1½ cups sugar
1 cup kosher salt
1 gallon ice

Ribs
1 full rack pork spare ribs, about 2½ pounds
¼ cub Rub Potion Number Swine (page 127)
⅓ cup Sweet Barbecue Sauce (page 128)

To make the brine, in a 10-quart pot, bring the water to a boil, then turn off the heat. Add the sugar and salt and stir until dissolved. Pour in the ice to chill the mixture. If you'd rather not bother with the ice, make the brine with 2 gallons of water, and do it far enough in advance so it will be completely cooled before adding the raw ribs.

To make the ribs, brine the ribs overnight, or for at least 4 hours. Preheat a smoker to 250°F. Evenly coat the ribs with about 2 tablespoons of the rub on each side. Put them bone side down on the rack of the smoker, directly over the coals. Let them cook for 1 hour, then flip and cook for another hour.

Check the sag of the ribs with the bend test. To do so, take a pair of tongs held perpendicular to the rib bones and guide one arm of the tongs

continued

PORK SPARE RIBS, CONTINUED

under the rib rack. Do so carefully so as not to rough up the underside of the ribs too bad. Once the arm of the tongs is halfway up the rack, pinch down on the rack and lift the whole thing up. If the ribs don't bend at all, you still have a long way to go. The more tender they become, the more bend you'll see when performing this test. Once there's enough bend that a seam opens up, cracking the surface of the rib bark on the top side of the ribs, they're tender enough to wrap.

Once they've reached the proper sag, wrap the ribs in foil and place them back on the pit for at least another hour. Use the bend test to check for doneness and tenderness. Rewrap and continue cooking if needed.

Unwrap the ribs, lightly brush each side with half the barbecue sauce, and put them back on the pit for 10 minutes longer, until the surface of the ribs is browned.

To serve, cut through the rack between the rib bones. The bones will be easier to locate with the ribs turned upside down. Serve with the remaining barbecue sauce on the side.

SMOKED TURKEY BREAST

Makes 8 to 10 servings

Pete Jones raised chickens, turkeys, peacocks, and guinea hens. Cows and goats were on the land too. It seemed like anything that walked, flew, and took a dump, this man raised at some point. The chicken they ate in their house came from the yard. It was the same way with turkey. Just as with any animal we raised for consumption, I was taught how to go about killing them, cleaning them, and getting them ready to cook not because I wanted to learn, but rather because my granddaddy wanted me to learn, and probably figured he wouldn't have to do it if I knew how.

When my granddaddy would clean the turkeys, he would dip them down in scalding water to get the feathers off. Then he'd put some newspaper in a bushel basket and light it on fire. That was where he singed off the rest of the feather hair. It was so odd, because to watch it you would think a bushel basket would just catch on fire.

One day, Pete decided he needed a feather plucker, so he bought one. It's still sitting behind my aunt's house. It stands about three feet high. There is a squirrel cage on it with rubber knobs maybe three or four inches tall. Before you pluck the feathers, you dip the bird down in scalding water. Then, you hold it up against the spinning wheel, and it removes the feathers. Simple, right? The first time we used that thing, granddaddy said, "All right, we're going to kill the turkey." I went in the pen to get a turkey and hit it in the head to kill it. At that point, granddaddy was just standing there smoking cigarettes. He wanted me to do the plucking.

I dipped the turkey down in that scalding water in the pot and flipped the plucker on. I was real apprehensive about this thing, but I put the turkey down on there. Granddaddy's standing there, smoking and itching to be critical. He says, "You're beating the skin off of him." I tried again, and finally he's like, "Just get out of the way." He grabbed the turkey by the neck and the feet, cigarette hanging out of his mouth, and it was like he put it in a pitching machine. He set it on that wheel, which shot it up against the barn door of the chicken house about ten feet away. That turkey was launched. At no point was there an admission of a mistake. He just said, "Go pick it up." I was standing there trying not to laugh.

I'm telling you that story so you understand why we cook boneless turkey breasts at Sam Jones BBQ. I had enough of dealing with whole turkeys and their feathers in my childhood.

Back when we first thought about adding turkey to the menu at Sam Jones BBQ (we never cooked it at Skylight), all I could think about was my Grandmother Smith's turkey at Thanksgiving. You know, everybody with blue or purple hair cooks turkey in the oven until it's bone dry. You could throw it in a mud hole and it'd soak up all the water. Michael Letchworth tried to convince me otherwise. He smoked a turkey breast and brought it into the kitchen during recipe testing. I took a hamburger bun and added a swipe of mayo and a slice of turkey. After one bite, I told him, "I was wrong."

It's the easiest meat to cook in this book and maybe has the biggest payoff considering the minimal effort involved.

continued

SMOKED TURKEY BREAST, CONTINUED

1 whole turkey breast,
4 to 5 pounds, skin
removed

2 tablespoons Rub
Potion Number Swine
(page 127)

Preheat a smoker to 250°F. Sprinkle the turkey breast generously on all sides with the rub.

Place the breast on the rack and cook it for about 90 minutes, or until it gets the right mahogany color. We're not looking for jet black here. The internal temperature should be 130°F.

Wrap the turkey tightly in foil, flip it over, and place back in the smoker until the internal temperature is 165°F, 45 to 60 minutes longer.

Remove the foil and retain the collected juices. Let the turkey rest for 30 minutes. Slice, then pour the collected juices over the sliced meat. Serve.

1947 BURGER

Makes 1 burger

There were two other barbecue restaurants run by our family members in Ayden when Pete and Robert opened Skylight in 1947. Pete cooked up a great burger. In fact, he served a lot of things that weren't barbecue, as my dad explains:

> They felt like they were competing against two seasoned veterans in the barbecue business in a small town. And so, daddy sold everything. There were hotdogs, hamburgers, grilled cheese sandwiches, ice cream, milkshakes, orangeades—I mean, you name it, he sold everything. Barbecue was still his main squeeze.

If I had to guess, it was probably a plain patty with no seasoning on the flat top. We're not trying to replicate that, but this is our homage to Skylight and the fact that it didn't just serve barbecue.

Pete didn't switch from white bread to buns for the barbecue sandwiches until 1989. I assume he didn't bother with buns for the burgers at the beginning either. For the burger at Sam Jones BBQ, we use the same bun that the barbecue sandwich is served on, a Martin's potato roll, but go ahead and try it on two slices of cheap, white bread if you're yearning for the authentic 1947 experience.

5 ounces (80/20) ground chuck

Dusting of Rub Potion Number Swine (page 127)

1 slice American cheese, preferably not a plastic-coated single

1 Martin's potato roll, buttered on the cut sides

Squeeze each of ketchup and yellow mustard

2 slices dill pickle

2 slices red onion

Shredded iceberg lettuce

1 slice tomato

Press the beef into a 4½-inch patty that's about ½ inch thick. Place it in a cast-iron pan over medium-high heat. Season the patty with the rub and cook on one side for about 4 minutes. Flip and season the other side with the rub. Cook until just shy of the desired doneness—about 3 more minutes for medium. Top the burger, still in the pan, with the cheese slice and cook until the cheese is melted, about 1 minute, or less if you use a lid. Grill the cut side of the buttered bun lightly in the same pan while the cheese is melting.

Place the bun on a plate and add ketchup, mustard, and pickles, and then the burger patty on the bottom of the bun. Place the onions, lettuce, and tomato slice on top of the bun and add the top bun. Fold over and enjoy.

HOG HEAD COLLARDS

Serves 30 to 40

Michael and I went round and round about the collard recipe. When I was growing up, the only time vinegar was on the table was when collards were as well. I wanted to make a collard recipe geared for the eastern North Carolina palate that wouldn't require any extra dashes of vinegar. When we finally agreed we were not going to cheap out, he ended up developing the final recipe for these greens, so I'll let him tell you how they came about:

Your standard collards are the larger, tougher cousin of our regional cabbage collards. If you've had collard greens anywhere in the South, you likely didn't eat cabbage collards, and they probably had the stems mixed in. We wanted just the leaves because they take far less time to cook than the stems. If you buy cleaned collards from a food provider, they'll come with the stems cut up into the mix. We brought in some bulk collards and timed two people in our kitchen cleaning them. The labor costs just weren't feasible. We reached out to Samuel's uncle Benny Cox at the Collard Shack next to Skylight, and he agreed to clean the collards for us. They're grown in Ayden. He brings them to us a few times a week. They cost a little more, but the key ingredient was something we weren't using but still paying for.

Our hogs don't have enough room to hang with the heads still on in the cooler at Sam Jones BBQ. When we first got our hogs, the heads were already cut off, but we still paid for the whole hog, including the head. They didn't even deliver the heads. We figured we could use the heads to flavor the stock for the collards instead of not having them

continued

delivered at all. I guess we could have used pork shanks or some other cut, but we were already paying for the heads.

The hog heads are smoked before we make the stock. They provide a bold flavor to the dish. The rest of the seasonings do as well, which is the point. You won't need to add hot sauce or vinegar to the finished product because the collards are already seasoned. They're on the spicy side, and the flavors are all savory. We're proud of them because they're so good, and also because they were the first side that we developed specifically for Sam Jones BBQ. We created and developed this recipe. These collards are ours.

This recipe is for a whole hog party, so it makes a mighty big batch (see page 176 if you're in need of a smaller quantity of greens). It requires a large burner and a pot no smaller than 30 quarts. If you have an outdoor burner and a pot for turkey frying or crawfish boils, use that.

Stock

1 hog head

2½ gallons water

1 large red onion, quartered

1 head garlic, cut in half across the cloves

¼ cup kosher salt

¼ cup sugar

Collards

1 cup lard or bacon grease

8 pounds collard greens, stems removed

⅓ cup kosher salt

1 tablespoon ground black pepper

1¼ cups Eastern North Carolina Barbecue Sauce (page 129)

1½ cups apple cider vinegar

1 medium red onion, chopped

¼ cup Texas Pete Hot Sauce

¼ cup sugar

To make the stock, smoke the hog head for 6 or 7 hours. For obvious reasons, this is most easily done while cooking a whole hog. The cheek meat should be tender enough at this point to pull away from the bone. Cut the skin around the cheek and pull the cheek meat from the skull. Peel off the skin and discard it. There are also a couple nuggets of meat that can be pulled from the temple area. You should have about 1 pound of meat total. Set it aside.

Pour the water into a pot that holds at least 30 quarts. Bring the water to a boil, then turn the heat down to a simmer. Add the smoked pig head (but not the reserved cheek meat), onion, garlic, salt, and sugar. Bring up to a bare simmer. The mixture should not be brought to a boil. Look for a few bubbles coming to the top at a consistent basis and hold that temperature.

Simmer the stock for 2 hours. Strain the stock, reserving the stock and discarding everything else. Put the strained stock back into the large pot.

To make the collards, bring the stock back up to a simmer. Add the lard and the pulled meat reserved from the head, and mix to incorporate. Add the collard leaves to the stock in four batches. Stir the leaves in and allow them to wilt before adding the next batch.

Simmer the greens for 1 hour. Add the remaining ingredients, stir to combine, turn off heat, and let the greens sit for 15 minutes. Stir once more and serve.

BARBECUE BAKED BEANS

Serves 8 to 10

My great-uncle Gerald was a cook in the National Guard. I always remember that if we had a family event, he was going to bring baked beans. I took his recipe and made it my own. His called for Kraft barbecue sauce and some other stuff. We have our own barbecue sauce at Sam Jones BBQ, and our beans are meatier. My daddy still prefers Uncle Gerald's recipe. He swears it's better than mine, Kraft barbecue sauce and all. Everyone has the right to be wrong.

½ pound (80/20) ground beef

¼ bell pepper, cut into ¼-inch dice

½ small red onion, cut into ¼-inch dice

2 (15-ounce) cans pork and beans, drained

1 cup Sweet Barbecue Sauce (page 128)

Preheat the oven to 375°F.

In a large pan over medium-high heat, brown the ground beef together with the bell pepper and onion. Cook the beef all the way through while stirring to break the beef into chunks. The onion and pepper should be wilted. Drain the fat off the beef once it's done.

Pour the beef mixture into a 9 by 13-inch baking dish or a dutch oven. Add the beans and barbecue sauce and mix well. Bake uncovered for 40 minutes. Serve immediately.

FOR A WHOLE HOG PARTY

Makes 70 to 80 servings

4 pounds (80/20) ground beef

2 bell peppers, cut into ¼-inch dice

4 small red onions, cut into ¼-inch dice

2 (114-ounce) #10 cans pork and beans, drained

8 cups (64 ounces) Sweet Barbecue Sauce (page 128)

PIMENTO CHEESE

Makes 1 quart

This is really the only recipe in this book that doesn't have a compelling backstory. Pimento cheese was something that was always in the fridge at my Granddad and Grandmother Jones's house, but we never had a secret family recipe. It's a good snack, and simple to make. You can also change it to your liking based on your favorite brand of mayo or hot sauce.

At Sam Jones BBQ, we serve pimento cheese with pork cracklins. Since we use all the skin in the barbecue, we have to order in dried pieces of pork skins. We call them "skin chips." They're thrown into a hot fryer for every order, and they puff up almost immediately. At home, feel free to put this stuff on any leftover pork skin from your whole hog party.

20 ounces mild cheddar cheese, grated

1 cup mayonnaise

½ teaspoon Texas Pete Hot Sauce

¼ teaspoon garlic powder

1½ cups diced pimentos

Place the grated cheese into a mixing bowl. In a separate bowl, mix together the remaining ingredients until combined. Pour over the cheese, then fold with a rubber spatula until combined.

SWEET POTATO MUFFINS

Makes 24 muffins

Either people are adamant about their love for our cornbread or they absolutely hate it. There is no middle ground. Younger people expect something fluffy and sweet, and our cornbread is exactly opposite of that. After it cools, it could go in your saddlebag and ride for days. There's nothing fluffy or sweet about it.

After we opened Sam Jones BBQ, we had lots of complaints about the cornbread from folks who had never had it at Skylight. I'd rather make a living than be right, so Michael and I starting working on an alternative. We tried a few recipes that weren't working out and were kind of at a loss about what to try next.

Kathy Diaz, who is one of the anchors in the SJB kitchen, overheard us talking about our search. She said she had a good recipe and made it for us. When the muffins came out of the oven, I brushed some melted butter on the top, and we tasted them. We had a winner. Butter makes everything better.

2 pounds sweet potatoes	½ cup unsalted butter, melted
¾ cup brown sugar	7 large eggs, beaten
1½ cups sour cream	3 cups self-rising cornmeal (see note)

Preheat the oven to 350°F.

Place the potatoes on a baking sheet and roast for 1 hour, until they are soft to the touch. When the potatoes are cool enough to handle, peel and mash them. Measure out 3 cups, and set the potatoes aside.

Raise the oven temperature to 375°F. Line the cups of two 12-cup muffin pans with paper or parchment liners.

Place the mashed sweet potatoes (warm from the oven or at room temperature) in a large bowl. Add the sugar, sour cream, and ¼ cup of the melted butter. Mix well. Add the eggs. Slowly add the cornmeal while mixing. Mix well until fully combined.

Pour the batter into the prepared muffin cups. Bake for 15 minutes, until the tops have browned. Brush the hot muffins with the remaining ¼ cup melted butter and remove from the pans to cool before serving. The muffins will keep, well covered, for a day or two.

NOTE: If self-rising cornmeal is not available, you can make your own by adding 1 tablespoon baking powder and ½ teaspoon salt to a 1-cup measuring cup, then filling it the rest of the way with cornmeal. That will equal 1 cup self-rising cornmeal.

Four

PIT RESURRECTION

Feasting on Tradition

There's a photo from the 1930s in the University of North Carolina archives. It captures a man standing next to a brick pit loaded with three whole hogs small enough they could be mistaken for lambs. A wooden structure surrounds the pit. There's a broom leaning against the wall, but no shovels in sight. The subject of the photo isn't mentioned in the simple caption: "Cooking barbecue in Ayden in the 1930s."

Emmitt Dennis at the old family pit in 1930—the same photo from the UNC archives.

John Shelton Reed sent me the photo in 2007 when he was doing research for *Holy Smoke*, his book on North Carolina barbecue. He thought I might know who the man was. My uncle Robert, Pete's brother, was still living, but he couldn't make out who was in the photo. He suggested I take it to Esther May Gibson, the daughter of Gracie and Emmitt Dennis, my triple great-aunt and -uncle. She was ninety years old at the time. Her vision wasn't what it once was. She found a few photos of her own for comparison, and finally said, "That's my daddy." It never dawned on me then to ask where the pit was.

Ten years later, on the way to the family cemetery, I went over to their old property to snoop around. Nobody was living at the house, which is within spitting distance of the Dennis family cemetery in Ayden where my grandparents are buried. Barns and outbuildings covered the property, many of them surrounded by overgrown weeds and vines. I had a hunch that the old pit might be back there because Emmitt Dennis used to live here, so I dodged some thorns and bent a sapling over to step through the open door of one wooden building. Old buckets, chairs, boxes, and scrap wood covered the floor. After digging around for a bit, I found a line of bricks stacked just a couple courses high. It was the top edge of the old barbecue pit. I couldn't see the rest because it was a trench dug into the ground. I had a lot of work ahead of me to uncover it.

Every bit of effort was worth it, and the work gave me some time to reflect. I grew up in a business that I didn't always appreciate and even grew to dislike. Through a series of events and opportunities, I came around and realized there was more to barbecue than providing me with employment. It's a legacy of eastern North Carolina and of my family that traces back long before me. My part of that legacy seemed pretty small as I stood in that old pit room, but with every shovelful of dirt, I became more grateful to be part of it now. Here I was, standing in front of a piece of family history, of barbecue history, with a deep appreciation that this pit waited long enough for me to come around.

I literally put blood, sweat, and a concussion into cleaning up that pit. A couple teenagers from the neighborhood came around and asked if they could help. We met one morning at the property. I told them, "If you boys think this is going to be easy money, you've come to the wrong place." Like an archeological excavation, I didn't want anything touched that absolutely didn't have to be. I had promised my relatives who own the property that no one would work on the property without me there. So, we went to work. I needed to get up on top of the building because the vines were so thick. I put one of the guys at the wheel of a front-end loader and got in the bucket. I tied myself off with some rope so that if everything fell apart I wasn't going to die. The kid in the driver's seat decided to pull up his phone and shoot a video of me up in the loader bucket clearing the vines, but that's not how I got a concussion.

I was standing on the bricks at the edge of the pit when one gave way, and I fell. I hit the ground hard. It was after hours, so I went to urgent care. The doctor looked me over and ran a CT scan. She said, "You've sustained a concussion." I didn't know exactly what that meant, but she told me to take it easy. I got up the next morning and went into the restaurant for a meeting. After the meeting, when I got up from the booth, I had a spell of dizziness that scared the hell out of me. Of course, I didn't go home and prop my feet up or anything. The next morning, I went to pull my boots on and fell headfirst onto the floor. It scared me so bad I immediately called my primary doctor. She said, "You have a concussion. You can keep trying to be Sam Jones, and it's going to take you a month to get over it, or you can do as I say. Go sit at home for a few days, and you'll most likely be back to normal by Monday."

She had told me not to do anything that required me to focus my eyes. This meant no computer, no cell phone. That four-day break was the longest I had unplugged from work in quite a long time. My mind, however, kept thinking about the possibility of cooking a pig on that old pit. It took some digging to deepen the pit and more than a little TLC on the brick and mortar surrounding the pit. The roof still leaks, and there are plenty of holes in the clapboard walls surrounding the building, but we got it ready for cooking.

On the morning of March 24, 2018, I banged the burn barrel with the side of a shovel to release some coals. The sun had not yet come up, so sparks from the burn barrel lit up the predawn sky as I carried the coals over to the pit. The coals I dropped in were the first to warm that pit in more than sixty years.

My great-great-uncle Emmitt Dennis cooked hogs on this pit for his restaurant in downtown Ayden, City Cafe. I don't know when the cooking operation was moved downtown, but the story is that my granddaddy started helping his uncle Emmitt when he was seven years old. That would have been in 1935, just five years after the photo of Emmitt beside this pit was taken. There's a good chance Pete Jones first learned how to cook barbecue on this pit. To resurrect that pit, to bring it back to life making barbecue for my community, was a powerful experience.

Connected to the old pit house is another rundown building, an annex. There's a rusted-out vat that's bolted to an old wooden table inside. We even found an ancient jar full of lard. This room was where the hogs were prepared for the pit. They were scalded, scraped, split, and hung. The hogs were slaughtered in another barn on the property and brought here. It was the last stop before they went on the barbecue pit.

Every time I've been on that property, I've thought about what it would be like to be present when they were butchering hogs in the room next to the pit. I wish I could go back for a day to watch Emmitt Dennis fire that pit, and see my granddaddy looking on, all the while knowing that to them, back then, this pit was nothing special. It was a way of life. A functional tool that allowed them to make a living. They probably never imagined it would become hallowed ground for a man four generations in the future.

The pit cooked well as soon as I added another course of loosely spaced bricks just below the lid. When we started, the sheet metal lids were sitting too tight to the top of the pit. It wasn't breathing. Half of the pit is belowground, and the part aboveground is a solid wall of brick and mortar. A standard block pit lets in a lot more air, which keeps the coals going. Those coals might not be actively producing flame anymore, but they still need oxygen to stay alive. Once we got that figured out, it was smooth sailing.

The hogs were beautiful. The color was perfect. It felt good to see that, knowing this was my maiden voyage with this pit. Once the skin was crisp, and all the photos and videos had been taken, it was time to serve.

You can be the best singer in the world, but if nobody's in the auditorium to hear you, you're not appreciated. Every time I was working on that property or cooking on that pit was special, but by having my friends and family there to enjoy it, to truly appreciate it, is something I'll never forget. Friends from across the country paused their lives to come share that day with me. It wouldn't have meant as much if I'd used that pit to cook a few hogs that I served back at Sam Jones BBQ. There would have been

some folks on Instagram who thought it was cool, but the experience of celebrating there, on this hallowed ground with my friends and family, tied a bow on it.

There are certain things that we as humans can do without, but love from another human is not one of them. If my restaurant went away, and I had to sell my house and my trucks, I would survive as long as I had friends and family around me.

The whole point of cooking a hog isn't just to have something to eat at the end. It's to have an excuse to bring your loved ones together to share a slice of your lives without distractions. A whole hog on a pit forces you to pause your other commitments in life and focus on what's in front of you. And in the end, it's not going to get eaten unless you have a crowd to share it with. I don't know how else to say it. Whole hog barbecue slows life down, brings folks together, and makes them smile. That's why it is my favorite kind of barbecue.

SHRIMP STEW WITH SCALLOPS

Makes 30 to 40 servings

My grandfather liked to invite his friends to his house. There were always anywhere from eight to fifteen people around the table on a daily basis. About once a month, he would invite so many that they filled the house.

My first recollection of this stew was at his home. The veneer-topped tables were set up in the living room. It was crowded. My cousin and I had our cowboy clothes on, and we put on a Western show. They clapped, and my grandfather asked me to sing a song. It was probably a church song, but I don't remember. This monthly dinner evolved to where his home couldn't accommodate it, so it moved to the side room of Skylight. There were at least fifty people, and only a small bowl of barbecue on the table. This was a seafood-centric meal. There was fish, and shrimp prepared so many ways you were bound to like one. However, his shrimp stew was the star of the show. There was more pork in the stew than offered on the table.

Pete would peel and dice potatoes. Then he'd cook the bacon off and use the grease in the stew. Then he'd cube the ham and put it in the stew. He was methodical and paid attention to the size and amount of everything. If it went into that stew, he wanted to touch it himself. It was the centerpiece for this dinner, which also included boiled shrimp, fried shrimp, and . . . now I'm starting to sound like Bubba Gump.

Anyway, the stew was special for him. He'd have a 60-quart pot of it. You don't have to make that much, but you don't make shrimp stew for two. There was always some left for people to take home and for us to eat for two or three days. My grandfather always prepared the same size batch. He'd hoist the giant pot right onto the table, with a ladle in the pot for everyone to serve themselves.

The memories shared at those times make the stew much more special than the recipe itself. He last made it the Christmas before he died. Gerald Pierce, my great-uncle and Pete's brother-in-law, helped him. He's the only one living who still knows how to make the stew, so I asked him to teach me. We spent a whole day cooking at my shop. I was so eager to learn. I would dare say I took more notes from him than any teacher I had in school.

After twenty-six years of cooking in the Army Reserve, Gerald is used to cooking in big batches and is well versed in cooking outdoors. This big batch requires a turkey fryer or crawfish pot set up with a propane burner and at least a 30-quart pot.

A note on the onions: Uncle Gerald is particular about his white onions. When each onion is halved, if any green is showing in the center, he carefully removes it. It's up to you if you want to bother with the extra step, but that's how Uncle Gerald would do it.

continued

2 pounds sliced bacon, cut into 1-inch pieces

1½ pounds country ham, cut into ¼-inch dice

2 gallons water

5 pounds white onions, cut into ½-inch dice

7 pounds russet potatoes, peeled and cut into ½-inch dice

10 pounds (28-count) shrimp, peeled and deveined

6 pounds medium-size sea scallops

Salt and pepper, for serving

Light a propane burner (outdoors!) and place a 15-inch or larger sauté pan, preferably cast iron, on the burner. Add the bacon and fry over medium-high heat. As the fat begins to render, stir the bacon. Continue to flip and stir the bacon until it's well browned, 10 to 15 minutes.

Drain the contents of the pan over a heatproof bowl, reserving the fat. Place the bacon aside. Pour the bacon grease back into the pan and add the ham. Fry the ham until it just begins to brown. Don't let the ham cook so long that it stiffens up, as it will be hard to eat in the finished stew. Once the ham is done, after about 10 minutes, drain the contents again. This time, discard the fat or keep it for frying eggs. Set the ham aside.

Pour the water into a pot that holds 30 quarts or more. Place it on the burner. Add the onions and bring the water to a rolling boil. It might take a while.

Once the water is boiling, add the potatoes, bacon, and ham, and bring back to a boil. Continue cooking until the potatoes are a little less than fork tender, about 15 minutes.

Add the shrimp and scallops and stir well. The water will stop boiling, and you don't want it to boil again. At this point, make sure all the ingredients are covered by the water. If not, add some hot water (preferably boiling water) until the ingredients are just covered.

Place the lid on the pot and wait 5 minutes. Stir again, bringing the shrimp and scallops into view at the top of the pot. It won't take long for the shellfish to cook through. Once the shrimp turn white and the scallops develop some cracks in their surface, take a couple out and test them for doneness. Both the shrimp and the scallops should be opaque all the way through when cut. Probably the longest they will take is 10 minutes of cooking. Once the shellfish is done, ladle the stew and some of the broth into bowls for serving immediately.

Salt and pepper should be on the table to season as required to individual tastes. The saltiness of the bacon and ham will vary, so it's best not to add salt too early. The stew will probably need some salt, but remember that Pete never would have reached for anything fancier than a shaker of table salt.

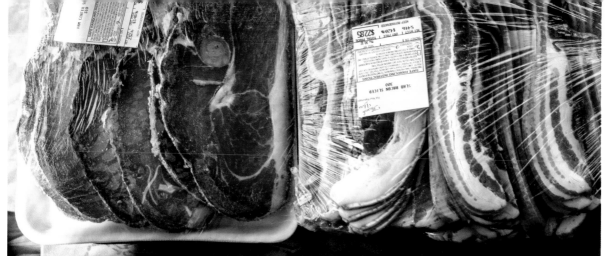

FISH STEW

Serves 15 to 20

In eastern North Carolina, there are two different fish stews—a white and a red. The difference is tomato in some form or fashion. Growing up, I preferred the red. This recipe is a hybrid that originated from Wanda Smith. She made cornbread at Skylight Inn for twelve years before she passed on. She'd make a fish stew about once a month for herself at Skylight and carry it home. One day, I offered to buy the fish if she'd show everyone at the store how to prepare the stew. The recipe below was fine-tuned in my barn by Michael Letchworth, who makes it for random get-togethers.

The stew can be made with different varieties of fish. Rock is a popular fish for stew in our part of North Carolina, but it's got a lot of bones, which I don't like. I said this was a hybrid. Thanks to Letchworth, catfish bellies are my choice, but fillets will also work. I added the eggs. We crack a couple dozen right into the pot at the end. Wanda wasn't a fan of the eggs, but she was used to me doing things she didn't approve of.

Ayden is the home of Carolina Classics Catfish. It's dang good farm-raised catfish, but being from the area, I always took the business for granted. The first time I met my friend and chef Ashley Christensen of Raleigh, North Carolina, she was cooking this same catfish at Charleston Wine + Food. That in itself makes this stew a little more fancy.

This is still the down-market cousin to the pricier Shrimp Stew with Scallops on page 167. Make that one on special occasions, whereas this stew feeds a crowd for a bargain. We cook it all the time while out on the road at barbecue festivals when the last thing you want to share with pitmasters is more barbecue. It goes well with some crusty bread for sopping.

1 pound sliced bacon, cut into 1-inch pieces

1 pound fresh sausage links, cut into 1-inch pieces

4 medium red onions, roughly chopped

¾ cup (one 6-ounce can) tomato paste

5 pounds red potatoes, unpeeled, cut into ¼-inch-thick slices

4 cloves garlic, chopped

1 gallon chicken stock

2 quarts water

1 teaspoon ground black pepper

3 tablespoons table salt

½ teaspoon chili powder

1 tablespoon ketchup, plus more for serving

5 pounds catfish bellies or fillets, cut into 1-inch pieces

18 large eggs

Texas Pete Hot Sauce, for serving

Light a propane burner (outdoors!) and place a pot that holds at least 20 quarts on the burner.

Add the bacon and sausage and fry over medium-high heat. As the fat begins to render, and enough fat has collected at the bottom of the pot, add the onions. Continue to stir until the bacon and sausage are browned and the onions are cooked through, about 15 minutes.

Add the tomato paste and stir until it thoroughly coats the ingredients in the pan. Add the potatoes, garlic, stock, water, pepper, salt, chili powder, and ketchup. Make sure to scrape the bottom of the pan to release any good brown bits that have built up. Bring to a boil and cook until the potatoes are fork tender, 10 to 15 minutes.

Once the potatoes are done, add the fish and *do not stir*, so the pieces of fish remain intact. Simmer for 5 minutes, until the fish has turned white and flaky.

continued

FISH STEW, CONTINUED

Crack all the eggs directly into the stew and *do not stir.* Once the eggs are poached, after about 5 minutes, turn off the heat and serve immediately.

Dip a ladle deep into the stew and pull it straight up out, snagging an egg along the way. If a guest doesn't like eggs, the way they are poached in the liquid makes them easy to avoid. Serve the hot sauce (and some ketchup for those who prefer it sweeter) on the side for folks to add as many dashes as they prefer.

COUNTRY-STYLE STEAK AND GRAVY

Serves 4 to 8

My mom, Judy, started at the telephone company right out of high school as an operator. She retired as a fiber optics engineer with forty-three years of service to the company.

While I was growing up, my dad was gone a lot for church-related stuff. My mom didn't get off work 'til five o'clock, but she'd have a full spread every night for me and my two sisters. Even homemade biscuits were on the table. If I were sentenced to the electric chair tomorrow, I'd want my mom's country-style steak and gravy, mac and cheese, biscuits, and Biscuit Pudding and Chocolate Gravy (page 185) as my last meal on earth.

The country-style steak is one of the simplest things ever, and I'm not embarrassed a bit about it. The gravy is just hot water, flour, and onion soup mix. Just like our family, there's nothing pretentious about it.

¾ cup all-purpose flour

4 cups hot water

1 (2.2-ounce) packet Lipton Beefy Onion soup mix

2 tablespoons vegetable oil

8 eye of round steaks, each about 8 ounces and ½ inch thick

Salt and freshly ground black pepper

In a jar or other container with a tight-fitting lid, combine the flour, water, and soup mix. Shake vigorously to combine and set aside.

In a 15-inch skillet, preferably cast iron, over medium-high heat, heat the vegetable oil. (If you have a smaller skillet, fry the steaks in batches.) Dry the steaks off with a paper towel, then sprinkle both sides of the steaks with salt and pepper. Place in the hot skillet and sear both sides of the steaks, pressing down on them as they cook if necessary, for 3 to 4 minutes per side. Remove the steaks from the pan. Do not wipe out the pan.

Turn the heat to medium, shake the flour and water mixture again, and pour into the skillet. Using a wooden spoon or heavy whisk, stir the mixture and scrape up any brown bits left from the steak to combine them with the gravy. Cook for 1 to 2 minutes, allowing the flour to cook a bit and the gravy to become thick. Add more water if needed to achieve a dense gravy. Add salt and pepper to taste.

Turn the heat to low and add the steaks back into the skillet, spooning over some of the gravy to keep the meat moist. Cook, uncovered, for another 15 to 20 minutes, until the steaks are fork tender, spooning the gravy over the steaks every now and then. The meat will continue to release juices into the gravy and help create a rich and flavorful gravy. Serve hot with plenty of gravy covering the steaks.

CABBAGE COLLARDS

Serves 10 to 15

Uncle Robert would invite a bunch of people to his house for dinner on Tuesdays. It was once or twice a month, but I wasn't invited to start with. I think he just didn't think about me. One day he was standing in his yard with a rifle in his hand. I walked over and asked him what was going on. He told me, "The dang squirrels are eating up my pecans, and I can't see good enough to shoot them." I said, "Give me the rifle." He said, "I'll make you a deal. You shoot 'em and I'll clean 'em. When we get a mess of them, we'll cook them and get some people over here." I killed forty-two squirrels in his yard over about five weeks. From that point on, I was always invited to that dinner.

He cooked the squirrels together in a big pot, and we invited everyone over. There've got to be at least 215 bones in a squirrel. There's a lot of work for little reward in those critters, which is why I'm not going to bother with a recipe for squirrels in gravy. But he always had cabbage collards on the table along with them. We'd spice them up with pepper vinegar. We also had slaw, potato salad, rutabagas. It was a big old country spread.

You may never have heard of cabbage collards because they were developed in North Carolina and are only grown commercially in the area surrounding Ayden. Cabbage collards are like a different vegetable from the regular collards you'll find at the local Piggly Wiggly. Instead of big, tough, green leaves, cabbage collards are more tender with lighter coloration. They have cabbage-like layers of leaves that are harvested by peeling them away from the center and leaving the bulb to create more leaves.

The collards are the specialty of the Collard Shack, which sits next door to the Skylight Inn. It is run by my dad's first cousin, Vickie Cox, and her husband, Benny. We call him Uncle Benny, and he explained how cabbage collards change throughout the growing season:

In the summer, the collards are tougher. When the cold weather starts, the leaves twist up on themselves like a cabbage. The more frost and cold that comes, the sweeter and more tender the cabbage collards get. The winter collards take less time to cook. When we cook collards, we'll use corned pig tails or some side meat. Some people use the aitchbone out of a ham or ham hocks. Anything that's smoked will work.

This recipe is for the sweet, tender winter collards. You'll only be able to find them in our area of North Carolina, preferably purchased from the Collard Shack. We apologize for the inconvenience, but it's one more reason you should drop by Ayden for a taste of our barbecue.

continued

CABBAGE COLLARDS, CONTINUED

2 quarts water

1-pound piece of slab bacon or 2 ham hocks

10-ounce piece of salt-cured pork side meat (unsmoked bacon), cut into chunks

5 pounds winter cabbage collards, stems removed and leaves roughly chopped

½ cup bacon grease or other animal fat, such as lard

1 red bell pepper, diced

Salt and pepper to taste

Boil the water in a pot that holds at least 8 quarts. Add the bacon and pork. Simmer, covered, for 90 minutes.

Wash the collards thoroughly, two or three times, in a clean sink full of water. Add them to the pot along with the bacon grease and the bell pepper. Add salt and pepper to taste.

Boil for about 30 minutes, uncovered, stirring occasionally, until the collards are tender. Serve.

PIG PICKIN' CAKE

Makes one 9-inch cake, 8 to 12 servings

A pig pickin' cake might be unfamiliar to you, but in eastern North Carolina, everybody knows what it means. It's a layer cake with pineapple icing and mandarin oranges in the cake. It shows up at every family gathering, and at the local church homecoming there are at least three or four pig pickin' cakes.

This one uses a box mix. The recipe might have originated with my grandma, and she certainly made it from scratch to begin with, but she had a job keeping an eye on Pete's tropical fish business and also made three meals a day. My parents were raised during the age of convenience. Microwave dinners and box mixes were the future. Also, my mom had an eight-hour-a-day job. If she got home at 5:00 p.m. and had a cake ready after dinner, you better believe it was coming from a box mix.

I have a recipe that's from scratch and was passed down from my great-grandma. I've always felt that, in true fashion, she purposely left a little detail or two out because she wouldn't have wanted anyone thinking theirs was as good as hers. Someone will challenge me on this, but we made both for a real live pig pickin' taste test, and the box mix version won hands down. Besides, you'll also have a whole hog to tend to, so accept any shortcuts you can find for preparing all the trimmings.

Cake

2 boxes yellow cake mix

6 large eggs, lightly beaten (or as instructed on the package)

⅔ cup vegetable oil (or as instructed on the package)

1 (15-ounce) can mandarin oranges, with juice

Icing

2 (3-ounce) boxes instant vanilla pudding

2 (8-ounce) containers Cool Whip

1 (15-ounce) can crushed pineapple, drained

To make the cake, preheat the oven to 350°F. Grease and flour three 9-inch cake pans.

Prepare the cake mixes according to the package directions, which will probably call for eggs and vegetable oil. Fold in the mandarin oranges with their juice. Pour the batter evenly into the prepared pans.

You may have a little batter left over. You can make some cupcakes or a smaller layer for tasting.

Bake for 25 to 35 minutes, or according to the cake mix directions, or until a toothpick inserted into the center of a cake comes out clean. Cool the cakes in the pans for 5 minutes, and then turn out onto racks to cool completely.

To make the icing, in a large bowl, mix the instant pudding and Cool Whip together. Stir in the pineapple.

Set one layer on a plate and spread with the icing. Add a layer and spread with icing. Add the final layer and spread with icing. You can keep the sides bare (think of this as showing the "bones" of the cake) or spread the icing all over the cake to completely cover. The cake can me made several hours ahead and chilled, but is ideally served at room temperature.

BISCUIT PUDDING
WITH CHOCOLATE GRAVY

Serves 12 to 15

The best thing my grandmother gave to my mom, including my dad, is the recipe for her biscuit pudding. The best thing mom ever made, besides me, is this biscuit pudding with chocolate gravy. I haven't found the verse yet, but I think somewhere the Bible says that biscuit pudding was really the reason that Lazarus was raised from the dead. My mom also made a chocolate gravy that she poured over the top. That also may have been what Jesus rubbed on the blind man's eyes.

Grandma Jones didn't make this dessert all the time, but when she did, she'd always send me home packing a big square of it. I once took it to school to eat at lunch. A few at my table were curious about it, and asked for a taste. I actually got in a little trouble for trying to share that biscuit pudding—for fifty cents a square. The administration wasn't having it—something about a noncompete clause—so I had to stop. It was an early taste of being an entrepreneur.

Pudding

3 (9.5-ounce) cans Butter-Me-Not Biscuits or any canned biscuit with "butter" or "buttery" in the description

4 cups whole milk, at room temperature

1 cup salted butter, melted

4 cups sugar

5 large eggs, at room temperature

1 teaspoon ground nutmeg

1 teaspoon vanilla extract

Chocolate Gravy

¼ cup cocoa powder

1 cup sugar

3 tablespoons all-purpose flour

Pinch of kosher salt

2 cups whole milk

¼ cup cold salted butter, cubed

To make the pudding, crack the biscuit cans open on the edge of the counter. I thought it was so cool when my mom did that. Bake the biscuits according to the instructions on the can.

Set the oven temperature at 350°F. Grease a 9 by 13-inch baking pan.

Combine the milk, butter, sugar, eggs, nutmeg, and vanilla in the bowl of a stand mixer or food processor. Mix to combine. Crumble the biscuits by hand into the mixture. Continue to mix until relatively smooth. Pour into the prepared pan.

Bake for 45 minutes, or until the pudding is stiff and lightly browned on top.

While the pudding is baking, make the gravy. Sift the cocoa, sugar, flour, and salt together into a 12-inch skillet. Slowly pour in the milk, while whisking, and continue to whisk until the mixture is smooth.

Cook over medium-high heat, while stirring, until the gravy thickens to the consistency of a thin pudding, about 8 minutes. Take the pan off the heat and add the cubed butter. Stir until the butter is melted and the gravy is smooth.

To serve, place a scoop of pudding into each bowl and top with a ladleful of gravy.

RESOURCES

BQ Grills

If you have some disposable income and would like a more permanent pig cooker than the block pit featured in these pages, order one of BQ cookers we use in our restaurants. Make sure to get the charcoal/wood burning version, not the gas one.

bqgrills.com

Thermoworks

We use the Thermapen instant-read thermometer to check the progress of our hogs in the cooker. They're accurate and superfast so you don't need to leave the lid open too long to get your readings.

thermoworks.com

Bar-B-Q Pigs, LLC

Owner Jay Black and his family have delivered hogs to us since the 1970s. Based in Wilson, North Carolina, they offer whole pigs from 30 to 250 pounds.

bbqpigsinc.com

Carolina Classics Catfish

This is where we get our catfish nuggets for the restaurant and catfish bellies for the fish stew recipe (page 171). There's no cleaner-tasting catfish around, and they're farmed right here in Ayden, North Carolina.

cccatfish.com

The Collard Shack

Bennie and Vicki Cox sell their famous cabbage collards from this shack that shares a parking lot with Skylight Inn. They don't have a website, so you'll have to visit on a Thursday, Friday, or Saturday when they're open for business. Meeting Uncle Benny will be the highlight of your visit.

Sumrell's Country Sausage

If we need bacon, sausage, ham hocks, country ham, or side meat, we get it from this meat market that's been serving our community for decades.

facebook.com/pages/Sumrells-Country-Sausage/155648527809235

Cheerwine

We were proud that Skylight Inn was among the first restaurants in Eastern North Carolina to ever have Cheerwine hooked up to the drink machine. Whether traveling, or at home, I am often found with one in my hand. I never leave North Carolina without it.

cheerwine.com

Texas Pete

Since day one, Skylight has used Texas Pete Hot Sauce. Family owned, and based in central North Carolina, it, too, accompanies me whenever there is an event with my name on it.

texaspete.com

Yeti

I've always been a fan of Yeti. They produce great products that live up to what they preach. They even make coolers big enough to transport up to two whole hogs and camp chairs made for pulling an all-nighter cooking said hogs. On their website I am listed as a "Brand Ambassador." While I do believe in and stand behind the product, my relationships with folks at Yeti are much more valuable to me. These are my kind of people.

yeti.com

Buffaloe Milling Company, Inc.

These folks in Kitrell, North Carolina, make the Moss Light n' Sweet Hushpuppy Mix. You can use it to make hushpuppies, but it's the secret ingredient in our cornbread (page 38).

buffaloemilling.com

Sam Jones BBQ/Skylight Inn Supplies

We sell bottles of our sauces and rubs, along with plenty of hats and shirts, online. If you'd rather get them alongside a barbecue sandwich, stop in at Sam Jones BBQ in Winterville or Skylight Inn in Ayden and get your supplies right at our front counter.

samjonesbbq.com

ACKNOWLEDGMENTS

I believe writing this part was harder than the book itself. To think back on everyone who had a hand in this would take up more pages than I have been given.

First off, thanks to the man above for sparing me on so many occasions when I should have left this side. I have been given much more than I deserve. Second, thanks to my wife, Sarah, and two daughters, Elaina and Eliza. You three sacrifice more than anyone, and are never center stage to take any credit. Sarah, thank you for being you, a wonderful help-meet and mother. You are always understanding about all that comes with this traveling circus. I can promise you there's a place in heaven for you in return for putting up with me all these years! It will take a long time for our girls to understand how good their mother is. Elaina and Eliza, you girls are two of the reasons I do what I do. Always know, wherever I may be, that I love you girls more than my feeble vocabulary will allow me express. It is my hope that all we have sacrificed will be worth it.

Mom and Dad, thank you for doing your best to raise me to be who I am. I know we haven't always seen eye to eye, but know I am forever thankful, and in your debt. Though I have a little gray in my hair now, I have not forgotten the lessons of my youth about how to love, and how to treat others with kindness. I love and respect you both.

All of my grandparents have now passed on, but I'd be remiss to act as though they did not have an impact. I sure wish they could see this. To Pete and Lou Jones and Travis and Louise Smith: Thank you for being the giants you were in my life.

To the Southern Foodways Alliance and John T. Edge: As I've written here, if it were not for this organization and this man, no one would know who this Sam Jones guy is. I will always cherish my relationship with you, John T., and I'll always hold the SFA in the highest regard.

Nick Pihakis: You encouraged me, pushed me, and leveraged yourself personally to help Sam Jones BBQ to become a reality. I will never forget your kindness, friendship, and personal commitment to making sure Michael and I were successful.

Jeff and Bruce Jones (Bruce is different than Dad): Since grandad passed, we have been on quite a ride these last 14-plus years. I appreciate you trusting me to operate a restaurant so many in our family worked hard to build. It was left up to us not to let the torch die down. Even when we didn't know what we were doing, or why it wasn't working, we did it together. Thanks to both of you for your support.

To the Skylight Inn crew: The gang here never cuts anyone any slack. This especially applies to me. They also rarely let anyone down. There are a few names here that many of you may not know. These are people who stand just out of the spotlight, yet make the spotlight, and the person standing in it, shine. There would be no book, Skylight Inn, or Sam Jones BBQ, were it not for the efforts of you guys, year after year. Will Stafford, Aaron Jesmer, and yes, even you (Cousin) Steve Jesmer, thank you for what you do every day to make sure what started 70-plus years ago is better than ever. Especially when I throw a wrench in your plans by packing last minute for an event!

This includes you, Mike "Chopper" Parrott. I have never asked anything of you that you not only did, but did well. It slipped my mind the night of the pit resurrection to recognize all of your efforts to make that event come together. Even with my lack of communication, you had a very large part making that a memorable success for me and many others.

Chase Cayton, since your accident in 2015, you haven't physically been there every day as before. But, my friend, you will always be one of the family at Skylight Inn. I will never forget your contributions to help build the team and reputation we have today.

It would be a rough road without you guys, and I know it. Love each one of you.

To the Sam Jones BBQ management team: Thank you, Michael Letchworth, Nick Haase, Marshall Stafford, Holt Phillips, Bryn Gifford-Ruiz, and Ian McMillian, our management team that executes whether or not I'm there. Thank you for making our guests feel welcomed, and serving our food as best as it can be. You are all class.

Those first blurry months of opening SJB was an experience I will never forget. You have chosen to remain even when we really had no clue what challenge tomorrow would bring. For anyone to remain at a restaurant for over three years is quite rare. Words will not allow me to convey how much I appreciate and respect you for your loyalty, hard work, and support since day one. Thank you, Holt Phillips, Bryn Ruiz-Gifford, Thomas Butler, Amber Guthrie, Jason Jesmer, Garrett Payne, Tyler Letchworth, Lavelle Burney, Harrison Thompson, Kathy Diaz, Megan Jones, and Purvis Cohens.

Angie Mosier has lent me too many talents to name. Aside from being an outstanding book stylist, she is my friend. A friend I had to argue with just to reimburse her for travel and expenses for being a part of this (which still irritates me). However, I love her too much to be mad. Thank you, Miss Angie.

David Hale Smith, thank you for helping me realize this was even a possibility. I thought you were crazy when we met in New York years ago to talk about a book. So many have helped this turtle up on the fence post.

A huge thank you to my editor, Emily Timberlake. I couldn't imagine having to deal with me trying to write a book. You managed to do it and remain to be friends with me. Betsy Stromberg, you did an amazing job with the interior design. The whole gang at Ten Speed Press helped create something special for me between the covers on this project.

To my friend Denny Culbert: I never thought when we met years ago via SFA that you would be photographing my book! I really did not think you, me, your pal, Joe Vidrine, and Daniel Vaughn would hit it off to be great friends. Not to mention the extremely late nights in my barn, which didn't help my position with Sarah! Who knew we could close two of Vivian's restaurants, and still rally a late-night hodgepodge band (in which Denny played the volume knob)?

Daniel Vaughn, I'll never forget the first time we met, your first visit to Skylight. You and a photographer expected to find me as a silhouette standing in a doorway of a legendary smokehouse, not thigh-deep in a mud-filled trench, fixing water lines, and in a state of hating what I did for a living! We became friends via our sarcastic way of communicating. The rest has been history. Thank you for helping me craft this story in way that did it justice. I value our friendship more than you know.

Thank you to my sister, Sarah, for letting this (ragtag) team occupy your home when we were working on this project. You always said yes to my last-minute texts. Your hospitality was unmatched. The stories that we all have are ones for the books.

I never thought I'd get to meet anyone considered "famous" in any industry. To become true friends with real people who are viewed that way is actually way cooler. Thank you to each one of my friends who took the time to write a few kind words included in these pages. You people inspire me on so many levels, both professionally and personally.

To the "Barn Crew": We have been friends longer now than we have not. All those nights we hung out as young boys just sitting in my barn talking trash, or the weekend four-wheeler rides, morphed into lifelong friendships that can never be broken. You guys have always been there when I needed you, regardless of the situation. You have been called on for everything from "grab some ice on your way out here," to the much-hated words "I need a hand, I promise it won't take long" (which we all know is false), to being asked to be a pallbearer in what seemed to be the worst thing any of us had faced to date. Jason "Fig" Worley, Clay Johnston, Jeremy Cleaton, Chad White, Justin "Fuzzy" Dixon, Marcus Jones, Matt Wade, Michael Letchworth, and Jamie Smith, I couldn't fathom anyone having a better group of friends at home than we do.

Michael Letchworth: The journey we've been on is one that could have its own story. I have watched you grow up. You have become a man that many would aspire to be. At every turn, I knew you would always have my back at the end of the day. To have the opportunity to write a book is something. To actually do it much more painstaking than I ever thought. To summarize a friendship that spans almost half of my life in a paragraph or two is simply impossible. You have been a friend, a confidant, a brother, and always someone I could count on and trust. We have always been in each other's corner. I'm not known for always making wise decisions. However, the day I called you about us becoming partners was one of the best decisions I have ever made. You are cut from a cloth that I'm not sure is even made anymore. I wish I had been as smart as you when I was your age. I look forward to what the future has in store. Love you buddy.

To the people who come to our restaurants and events around the country, my mind continues to be blown when someone wants to talk to me because they appreciate the food that was served. I will always be the same person everywhere I go, and will never forget the little place I came from that I call home. My home is Ayden, North Carolina.

INDEX

A

Apple, R. W., Jr., 102
Atlanta History Center, 103

B

Back Roads America, 19, 20
Bacon
    Cabbage Collards, 176–78
    Fish Stew, 171–72
    Shrimp Stew with Scallops,
      167–68
Banana Pudding, Mama's, 47
Barbecue, definition of, 1–2
Barbecue Bowl, 21
Barbecue sauces
    Eastern North Carolina Barbecue
      Sauce, 129
    Sweet Barbecue Sauce, aka "Bean
      Sauce," 128
Bar-B-Que Pigs, 58
BBQ Pitmasters (TV show), 115
Beans, Barbecue Baked, 143
Beef
    Barbecue Baked Beans, 143
    Country-Style Steak and Gravy, 175
    1947 Burger, 136
Big Apple BBQ Block Party, 32, 106,
    112–13

Biscuit Pudding with Chocolate
    Gravy, 185
Black Bear, 112
Block, Ira, 19
Blue Smoke, 112
Bowen, Glenn, 101
BQ Grills, 57
Bringle, Carey, 112–13
Brock, Sean, 111
Burger, 1947, 136
Burn barrels, 60–61, 66, 68–70

C

Cabbage
    Sweet Coleslaw, 37
Cabbage Collards, 176–78
Cake, Pig Pickin', 180
Callaghan, Kenny, 112, 113
Capital Q (film), 32, 106, 111
Charleston Wine + Food, 106,
    113, 171
Cheese, Pimento, 146
Chicken and Sauce, Eastern North
    Carolina–Style, 41–42
Chocolate Gravy, Biscuit Pudding
    with, 185
Christensen, Ashley, 111, 171
City Cafe, 15, 160
Coleslaw, Sweet, 37

Collard greens
    Cabbage Collards, 176–78
    Hog Head Collards, 139–40
Collard Shack, 139, 176
Cornmeal
    Old-Fashioned Cornbread, 38
    Sweet Potato Muffins, 149
Country-Style Steak and Gravy, 175
Cox, Benny, 139, 176
Cox, Vickie, 176

D

Dennis, Emmitt, 7, 15, 155, 160
Dennis, Gracie, 155
Dennis, John Bill, 7, 15
Dennis, Mantha, 32
Dennis, Skilton, 32–33, 34
Desserts
    Biscuit Pudding with Chocolate
        Gravy, 185
    Mama's Banana Pudding, 47
    Pig Pickin' Cake, 180
Diaz, Kathy, 149
Durney, Billy, 119

E

Eastern North Carolina Barbecue
    Sauce, 129
Eastern North Carolina–Style Chicken
    and Sauce, 41–42
Edge, John T., 106, 111
Edwards, McDonald, 18

F

Farmer, Ashley, 28–29
Farmer, Jim, 17, 114
FatBack Collective, 111
Fish Stew, 171–72

G

Gibson, Esther May, 155

H

Haire, John, 111
Ham
    Cabbage Collards, 176–78
    Shrimp Stew with Scallops, 167–68

Hilton Garden Inn, 60
Hog Head Collards, 139–40
House, Larry, 22
Howard, Vivian, 60
Howell, James, 30, 32
Hunt, James, Jr., 21

J

James Beard Awards, 102–3, 113
Jim 'N Nick's BBQ, 106, 111
Johnson, Gene, 21
Jones, Bruce, 6, 7, 8, 16–17, 21, 25, 35,
    41, 101, 102, 111, 121, 122
Jones, Jeff, 6, 7, 8, 17, 32, 35, 102, 103,
    116, 120
Jones, Judy, 175
Jones, Pete, 1, 7, 8, 15–22, 24–25, 33,
    35, 101, 102, 116, 122, 133, 136,
    160, 167
Jones, Robert, 7, 15, 17, 136, 176
Jones, Sarah, 2, 6, 29, 112, 120

L

Ledbetter, Leigh, 119
Letchworth, Michael, 6, 24, 61, 114–16,
    119, 120, 127, 128, 133, 139,
    149, 171
Link, Donald, 111

M

Mama's Banana Pudding, 47
Mandarin oranges
    Pig Pickin' Cake, 180
Martin, Pat, 111, 112–13, 119
Merril, Billy, 115
Mills, Buddy, 7
Mosier, Angie, 119
Muffins, Sweet Potato, 149

N

National Geographic, 19–21, 32, 33

O

O'Neill, Thomas, 19